Stupid CCIE Tricks Series v5.0 - Section 10: MPLS

By Johnny Bass

Copyright

Notice of Rights

Notice of Liability

Every effort was made to either create original content or use public domain reference materials (Requests for Comment (RFC), vender configuration references and the like) to help create this document. The goal is to help in the process of study for certification and not steal copy written materials. If by mistake such materials are found within this document, please notify the author and corrections will be made.

Trademarks

Many of the designations used by manufactures and sellers to distinguish their products are claimed as trademarks. Where those designations appear in this document, and the publisher was aware of a trademark claim, the designations appear as requested by the owner of the trademark. All other product names and services identified throughout this document are used in editorial fashion only and for the benefit of such companies with no intention of infringement of the trademark. No such use, or the use of any trade name, is intended to convey endorsement or other affiliation with this document. CCIE and Cisco are registered trademarks of Cisco Systems, Inc.

Table of Contents

Dedications

All my efforts are for my family...my wife, Tiffany, and children, Sean and Cayman.

Johnny Bass has been in the networking industry since the late 1980s, specializing on Cisco System products since 1990 and has worked extensively in the Aerospace, Health Care, and Service Provider industries, providing network design, education, and technical support expertise. Holding both CCIE and CCSI credentials, Johnny has a proven record of teaching and consulting on Cisco Routing, Switching, Design, Implementation, and Support. During his tenure as a Senior Instructor with Global Knowledge, Johnny has developed extensive experience teaching CCNP/CCNP-SP/CCVP/Cisco Nexus and CCIE R&S courses. This experience has also allowed him to excel in the role of Course Director and Subject Matter Expert, with technical responsibility for Global Knowledge's North American CCIE R&S curriculum and Service Provider Technical Segment, including the Cisco CCIE 360 program for Routing and Switching; IPv6 Fundamentals, Design and Development; Building Cisco Service Provider Next-Generation Networks, Part 1 and Part 2; Deploying Cisco Service Provider Network Routing; Deploying Cisco Service Provider Advanced Routing; Implementing Cisco Service Provider Next-Generation Core Network Services; Implementing Cisco Service Provider Next-Generation Edge Network Services. Johnny is the author of the CCIE Routing & Switching Written Exam Boot Camp currently running in Europe. Johnny is a Cisco 360 R&S Master instructor; the first to achieve this level outside of the organization that created the program. Johnny is the co-author of the version 5.0 of the Cisco 360 course content for the advanced workshop 1 (CIERS1) and advanced workshop 2 (CIERS2). He is also a regular speaker at Cisco Live/Networkers in the US. In addition to his teaching engagements, Johnny is the owner and President of Bass Consulting Services, Inc., a network engineering consultancy based outside of Seattle, WA specializing with service provider and large enterprise networks for design, configuration, and troubleshooting support. Johnny lives in Gig Harbor Washington with his wife (Tiffany) and children (Sean and Cayman).

Brief

From Cisco's web site:

"The Cisco Certified Internetwork Expert (CCIE) certification is accepted worldwide as the most prestigious networking certification in the industry. Network Engineers holding an active Cisco CCIE certification are recognized for their expert network engineering skills and mastery of Cisco products and solutions. The CCIE community has established a reputation of leading the networking industry in deep technical networking knowledge and are deployed into the most technically challenging network assignments.

The program continually updates and revises its testing tools and methodologies to ensure unparalleled program quality, relevance and value. Through a rigorous written exam and a performance based lab, the CCIE program sets the standard for internetworking expertise.

Cisco introduced the CCIE certification in 1993 to assist the industry in distinguishing the top echelon of internetworking experts worldwide. Today, CCIE certification holders represent less than 3% of all certified Cisco professionals and less than 1% of the networking professionals worldwide."

The estimated pass rate for first attempts is ~5-7%, for all attempts is about 26%*. There is no doubt that the CCIE practical exam is difficult. As an attempt to help in your endeavor to obtain your CCIE number, I have written a series of documents, titled lovingly "Stupid CCIE Tricks", which tries to touch on those items found on the blue print for the CCIE Route Switch practical exam. The idea behind these documents is rather than purchasing a complete book that tries to cover all topics, this is broken into major topics and you can purchase the topic that you need or would like to focus on now. All section may or may not be currently available and as the CCIE itself, things are always in work.

The series includes:

Stupid CCIE Tricks v5.0 - section 1: Numbers in Networking
Stupid CCIE Tricks v5.0 - section 2: Dynamic Multipoint VPN (DMVPN)
Stupid CCIE Tricks v5.0 - section 3: Layer 2
Stupid CCIE Tricks v5.0 - section 4: IGP – RIP
Stupid CCIE Tricks v5.0 - section 5: IGP – OSPF
Stupid CCIE Tricks v5.0 - section 6: IGP – EIGRP
Stupid CCIE Tricks v5.0 - section 7: BGP
Stupid CCIE Tricks v5.0 - section 8: Redistribution
Stupid CCIE Tricks v5.0 - section 9: IPv6
Stupid CCIE Tricks v5.0 - section 10: MPLS
Stupid CCIE Tricks v5.0 - section 11: Multicast
Stupid CCIE Tricks v5.0 - section 12: Security
Stupid CCIE Tricks v5.0 - section 13: Network Services
Stupid CCIE Tricks v5.0 - section 14: QoS

* Cisco does not official publish pass rates, the first attempt is an estimate and all attempts was published in Network World in 2006, so do not take those numbers as gospel.

Using this Document

This is intended for those that need addition work on MPLS as it relates to a CCIE level of study. This document is broken into phases, MPLS in the CCIE Exam, History, Operational Overview, Configuration, Troubleshooting Tips and CCIE like exercises...in other words how MPLS might apply in a CCIE exam type of scenario.

Objective

To become familiar more familiar with MPLS as it relates to the CCIE practical exam and potential CCIE tasks.

Introduction

Even though MPLS tends to be a service provider type of technology, there are more and more enterprise that are starting to implement their own MPLS cloud. It may be used in combination with BGP (which we will not go into great detail here about, see **Stupid CCIE Tricks, section 9: BGP** for more). Typically the best practices and common deployment limits how we use the protocol and one goal is to setup MPLS in the most simplistic way to make it more supportable...with that said, MPLS has the potential of being complicated, depending on features that needs to be implemented. Due to this practice in the industry, the less obvious features may be ignored; therefore CCIE Routing and Switching candidates are missing points on those features. You need to have a good understanding of how MPLS works and what the options are...and how to use them in ways they may not have been intended. This document will attempt to cover the general operation of MPLS, but also how MPLS may be used within the CCIE R&S practical exam based on the version 5.0 blue-print.
The goal is to give the candidate an understanding of how MPLS works and how they may be used within the CCIE R&S practical exam and therefore will help shorten the time spent configuring and troubleshooting MPLS within the exam. We will look at how MPLS can be used to support IPv4 with Layer 3 VPNs. We will look at the history of MPLS, how it relates to the CCIE R&S Exam, Operational Overview, Configuration, Troubleshooting Tips and CCIE like exercises...in other words how MPLS might apply in a CCIE R&S exam type of scenario.

Recommended Reading

MPLS Fundamentals (Cisco Press ISBN-13: 978-1-58705-197-5)

MPLS and VPN Architectures (Cisco Press ISBN-13: 978-1-58705-002-2)
MPLS and VPN Architectures, Volume II (Cisco Press ISBN-13: 978-1-58705-112-8)

Icons used within this Series

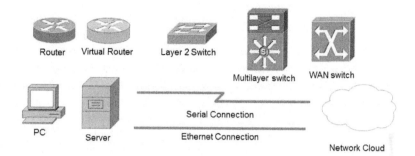

Router   Virtual Router   Layer 2 Switch

Multilayer switch   WAN switch

PC   Server   Serial Connection

Ethernet Connection

Network Cloud

Command Syntax Conventions

The conventions used to present command syntax in this document are the same conventions used in the IOS Command Reference. The Command Reference describes these conventions as follows:

- **Boldface** indicates commands and keywords that are entered literally as shown. In actual configuration examples and output (not general command syntax), boldface indicates commands that are manually input by the user (such as a show command).

- *Italics* indicate arguments for which you supply actual values.

- Vertical bars (|) separate alternative, mutually exclusive elements.

- Square brackets [ ] indicate optional elements.

- Braces { } indicate a required choice.

- Braces within brackets [{ }] indicate a required choice within an optional element.

History of Multiprotocol Label Switching (MPLS)

The original drivers towards label switching were designed to make routers faster in the forwarding process. In comparison, ATM switches were faster than routers; they used fixed length identifiers to make switching decisions. The thought was then that a fixed length label lookup would be faster than longest match used by IP routing. Therefore, allowing a device to do the same job as a router with performance of ATM switch. With enabling IP + ATM integration, the mapping of IP to ATM had become very complex, hence simplify by replacing ATM signaling protocols with IP control protocols.

In 1996 a group from Ipsilon Networks proposed a "flow management protocol". Their "IP Switching" technology, which was defined only to work over ATM, did not achieve market dominance. Cisco Systems introduced a related proposal, not restricted to ATM transmission, called "Tag Switching". It was a Cisco proprietary proposal, and was renamed "Label Switching". It was handed over to the Internet Engineering Task Force (IETF) for open standardization. The IETF work involved proposals from other vendors, and development of a consensus protocol that combined features from several vendors' work.

One original motivation was to allow the creation of simple high-speed switches, since for a significant length of time it was impossible to forward IP packets entirely in hardware. However, advances in the hardware technologies have made such devices possible. Therefore the advantages of MPLS primarily revolve around the ability to support multiple service models and perform traffic management. MPLS also offers a robust recovery frame word that goes beyond the simple protection rings of synchronous optical networking (SONET/SDH).

The first RFC that resembles MPLS came out in 1997 from Cisco on Tag Switching, RFC 2105 Cisco Systems' Tag Switching Architecture Overview. The RFC describes operation and terminology used by Cisco for Tag Switching. This was what was handed over to the IETF to be standardized. The terminology changed to match the term label, rather than tag. So the Tag Information Base (TIB) became the Label Information Base (LIB); the Tag Forwarding Information Base (TFIB) became the Label Forwarding Information Base (LFIP); the Tag Distribution Protocol (TDP) became Label Distribution Protocol. The first RFC that tries to define MPLS is RFC 3031 Multiprotocol Label Switching Architecture (2001), even though there are a couple RFCs that predates that RFC that describes Requirements for Traffic Engineering Over MPLS (RFC 2702 in 1999) and A Core MPLS IP VPN Architecture (RFC 2917 in 2000), the IETF were still working on the specification for MPLS.

Since RFC 3031, there have been several to add additional functionality to MPLS: RFC 3032 (January 2001) MPLS Label Stack Encoding.

- Updated by: RFC 4182, RFC 5332, RFC 5462.

RFC 3034 (January 2001) Use of Label Switching on Frame Relay Networks Specification.
RFC 3035 (January 2001) MPLS using LDP and ATM VC Switching.
RFC 3036 (January 2001) LDP Specification.
RFC 3063 (February 2001) MPLS Loop Prevention Mechanism.
RFC 3107 (May 2001) Carrying Label Information in BGP-4.
RFC 3270 (May 2002) Multi-Protocol Label Switching (MPLS) Support of Differentiated Services.

- Updated by: RFC 5462.

RFC 3353 (August 2002) Overview of IP Multicast in a Multi-Protocol Label Switching (MPLS) Environment.
RFC 3429 (November 2002) Assignment of the 'OAM Alert Label' for Multiprotocol Label Switching Architecture (MPLS) Operation and Maintenance (OAM) Functions.
RFC 3443 (January 2003) Time To Live (TTL) Processing in Multi-Protocol Label Switching (MPLS) Networks.

- Updates: RFC 3032 Updated by: RFC 5462.

RFC 3468 (February 2003) The Multiprotocol Label Switching (MPLS) Working Group decision on MPLS signaling protocols.
RFC 3469 (February 2003) Framework for Multi-Protocol Label Switching (MPLS)-based Recovery.

- Updated by: RFC 5462.

RFC 3471 (January 2003) Generalized Multi-Protocol Label Switching (GMPLS) Signaling Functional Description.

- Updated by: RFC 4201, RFC 4328, RFC 6003.

RFC 3472 (January 2003) Generalized Multi-Protocol Label Switching (GMPLS) Signaling Constraint-based Routed Label Distribution Protocol (CR-LDP) Extensions.

- Updated by: RFC 4201.

RFC 3473 (January 2003) Generalized Multi-Protocol Label Switching (GMPLS) Signaling Resource ReserVation Protocol-Traffic Engineering (RSVP-TE) Extensions.

- Updated by: RFC 4003, RFC 4201, RFC 4420, RFC 5420, RFC 6003.

RFC 3477 (January 2003) Signaling Unnumbered Links in Resource ReSerVation Protocol - Traffic Engineering (RSVP-TE).
RFC 3564 (July 2003) Requirements for Support of Differentiated Services-aware MPLS Traffic Engineering.

- Updated by: RFC 5462.

RFC 3811 (June 2004) Definitions of Textual Conventions (TCs) for Multiprotocol Label Switching (MPLS) Management.

RFC 3812 (June 2004) Multiprotocol Label Switching (MPLS) Traffic Engineering (TE) Management Information Base (MIB).

RFC 3813 (June 2004) Multiprotocol Label Switching (MPLS) Label Switching Router (LSR) Management Information Base (MIB).

RFC 3814 (June 2004) Multiprotocol Label Switching (MPLS) Forwarding Equivalence Class To Next Hop Label Forwarding Entry (FEC-To-NHLFE) Management Information Base (MIB).

RFC 3815 (June 2004) Definitions of Managed Objects for the Multiprotocol Label Switching (MPLS), Label Distribution Protocol (LDP).

RFC 3919 (October 2004) Remote Network Monitoring (RMON) Protocol Identifiers for IPv6 and Multi-Protocol Label Switching (MPLS).

RFC 3945 (October 2004) Generalized Multi-Protocol Label Switching (GMPLS) Architecture.

RFC 3946 (October 2004) Generalized Multi-Protocol Label Switching (GMPLS) Extensions for Synchronous Optical Network (SONET) and Synchronous Digital Hierarchy (SDH) Control.

RFC 4003 (February 2005) GMPLS Signaling Procedure for Egress Control.

RFC 4023 (March 2005) Encapsulating MPLS in IP or Generic Routing Encapsulation (GRE).
- Defines IP protocol 137 (MPLS in IP).
- Updated by: RFC 5332.

RFC 4105 (June 2005) Requirements for Inter-Area MPLS Traffic Engineering.

RFC 4126 (June 2005) Max Allocation with Reservation Bandwidth Constraints Model for Diffserv-aware MPLS Traffic Engineering & Performance Comparisons.

RFC 4127 (June 2005) Russian Dolls Bandwidth Constraints Model for Diffserv-aware MPLS Traffic Engineering.

RFC 4139 (July 2005) Requirements for Generalized MPLS (GMPLS) Signaling Usage and Extensions for Automatically Switched Optical Network (ASON).

RFC 4182 (September 2005) Removing a Restriction on the use of MPLS Explicit NULL.
- Updated by: RFC 5462.

RFC 4201 (October 2005) Link Bundling in MPLS Traffic Engineering (TE).

RFC 4202 (October 2005) Routing Extensions in Support of Generalized Multi-Protocol Label Switching (GMPLS).

RFC 4203 (October 2005) OSPF Extensions in Support of Generalized Multi-Protocol Label Switching (GMPLS).

RFC 4206 (October 2005) Label Switched Paths (LSP) Hierarchy with Generalized Multi-Protocol Label Switching (GMPLS) Traffic Engineering (TE).

RFC 4208 (October 2005) Generalized Multiprotocol Label Switching (GMPLS) User-Network Interface (UNI): Resource ReserVation Protocol-Traffic Engineering (RSVP-TE) Support for the Overlay Model.

RFC 4216 (November 2005) MPLS Inter-Autonomous System (AS) Traffic Engineering (TE) Requirements.

RFC 4221 (November 2005) Multiprotocol Label Switching (MPLS) Management Overview.

RFC 4247 (November 2005) Requirements for Header Compression over MPLS.

RFC 4257 (December 2005) Framework for Generalized Multi-Protocol Label Switching (GMPLS)-based Control of Synchronous Digital Hierarchy/Synchronous Optical Networking (SDH/SONET) Networks.

RFC 4258 (November 2005) Requirements for Generalized Multi-Protocol Label Switching (GMPLS) Routing for the Automatically Switched Optical Network (ASON).

RFC 4328 (January 2006) Generalized Multi-Protocol Label Switching (GMPLS) Signaling Extensions for G.709 Optical Transport Networks Control.

RFC 4364 (February 2006) BGP/MPLS IP Virtual Private Networks (VPNs).

- Obsoletes: RFC 2547.
- Updated by: RFC 5462.

RFC 4365 (February 2006) Applicability Statement for BGP/MPLS IP Virtual Private Networks (VPNs).

RFC 4368 (January 2006) Multiprotocol Label Switching (MPLS) Label-Controlled Asynchronous Transfer Mode (ATM) and Frame-Relay Management Interface Definition.

RFC 4377 (February 2006) Operations and Management (OAM) Requirements for Multi-Protocol Label Switched (MPLS) Networks.

RFC 4378 (February 2006) A Framework for Multi-Protocol Label Switching (MPLS) Operations and Management (OAM).

RFC 4379 (February 2006) Detecting Multi-Protocol Label Switched (MPLS) Data Plane Failures.

- Updated by: RFC 5462.

RFC 4385 (February 2006) Pseudowire Emulation Edge-to-Edge (PWE3) Control Word for Use over an MPLS PSN.

RFC 4397 (February 2006) A Lexicography for the Interpretation of Generalized Multiprotocol Label Switching (GMPLS) Terminology within the Context of the ITU-T's Automatically Switched Optical Network (ASON) Architecture.

RFC 4426 (March 2006) Generalized Multi-Protocol Label Switching (GMPLS) Recovery Functional Specification.

RFC 4427 (March 2006) Recovery (Protection and Restoration) Terminology for Generalized Multi-Protocol Label Switching (GMPLS).

RFC 4428 (March 2006) Analysis of Generalized Multi-Protocol Label Switching (GMPLS)-based Recovery Mechanisms (including Protection and Restoration).

RFC 4446 (April 2006) IANA Allocations for Pseudowire Edge to Edge Emulation (PWE3).

RFC 4448 (April 2006) Encapsulation Methods for Transport of Ethernet over MPLS Networks.

- Updated by: RFC 5462.

RFC 4461 (April 2006) Signaling Requirements for Point-to-Multipoint Traffic-Engineered MPLS Label Switched Paths (LSPs).

RFC 5317 (February 2009) Joint Working Team (JWT) Report on MPLS Architectural Considerations for a Transport Profile.

RFC 5331 (August 2008) MPLS Upstream Label Assignment and Context-Specific Label Space.

RFC 5332 (August 2008) MPLS Multicast Encapsulations.

RFC 5339 (September 2008) Evaluation of Existing GMPLS Protocols against Multi-Layer and Multi-Region Networks (MLN/MRN).

RFC 5439 (February 2009) An Analysis of Scaling Issues in MPLS-TE Core Networks.

RFC 5623 (September 2009) Framework for PCE-Based Inter-Layer MPLS and GMPLS Traffic Engineering.

RFC 6601 (April 2012) Generic Connection Admission Control (GCAC) Algorithm Specification for IP/MPLS Networks.

Currently in draft: Updates to LDP for IPv6 draft-ietf-mpls-ldp-ipv6-12 that could update RFC 5036 is approved.

The benefits of MPLS are:
- MPLS de-couples IP packet forwarding from the information carried in the IP packet header
    - Conventional IP routing forwards packets based upon the destination IP address in the IP header
- Allows new routing functionality - new forwarding paradigms not available with conventional IP routing
- MPLS today is the enabler for new functionality / services:
    - VPNs
    - Traffic Engineering

- o Layer 2 transport
- o Guaranteed bandwidth services
- o Multi-Protocol Lambda Switching

MPLS within the CCIE Routing and Switching Exam

Per Cisco CCIE Routing and Switching Lab Exam Topics (Blueprint) v5.0
The following topics are general guidelines for the content likely to be included on the lab exam. However, other related topics may also appear on any specific delivery of the exam. In order to better reflect the contents of the exam and for clarity purposes, the guidelines below may change at any time without notice.

3.1.a	Implement and troubleshoot MPLS operations	
	3.1.a (i)	Label stack, LSR, LSP
	3.1.a (ii)	LDP
	3.1.a (iii)	MPLS ping, MPLS traceroute
3.1.b	Implement and troubleshoot basic MPLS L3VPN	
	3.1.b (i)	L3VPN, CE, PE, P
	3.1.b (ii)	Extranet (route leaking)

Implement Multiprotocol Label Switching (MPLS)

If we consider this section as the base configuration of MPLS, the original intent for label switching, we can start with a discussion of what the core network would look like without label switching first.

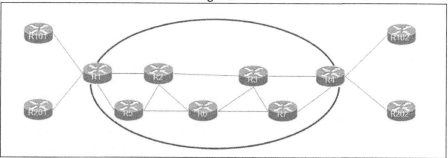

In the above diagram, we have a group of routers, where routers R1 through R7 are within the core of the network and R101, R102, R201 and R202 are outside of the core.

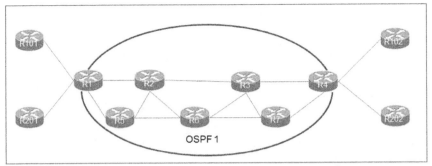

The core network is running OSPF, the edge routers (R1 and R4) are running another protocol or are using static routes, while the outside routers are using default routes pointed to the core. The edge routers would have to redistribute the routing or static routes related to the outside routers, so the rest of the core routers would be able to have reachability.

This presents a potential scalability issue within the core. All routers in the core would have to have a complete routing table (RIB) to be able to support all the traffic passing through the core. With this example, scale is not an issue, but if we started to grow this network to thousands of routers, the forwarding tables of the core routers would be fairly dramatic.

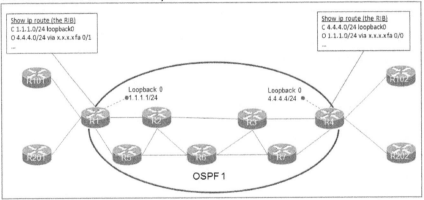

If we look at the subset of the routing table, we have learned routing information from the OSPF process and it's been selected as best and inserted into the RIB. Think back to the history section of this document, the original goal of tag switching and label switching was to simplify the process of forwarding traffic through a network. This does not reduce the size of the routing tables of the core routers, but rather change the method of forwarding the IPv4 traffic. Labels will be used, rather than using the IPv4 header. If the label is not useable, then the labels will be removed or popped and normal IPv4 forward will be used. To enable Multiprotocol Label Switching (MPLS) forwarding of IPv4 packets along normally routed paths for a particular interface, use the **mpls ip** command in interface configuration mode.

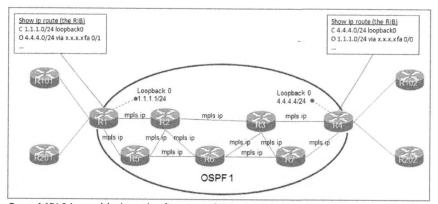

Once MPLS is enabled on the first interface, the label information based (LIB) is started. All routes within the RIB will have a label generated locally and placed into the LIB and referenced as local labels.

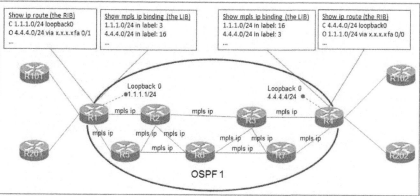

To display the LIB, use the **show mpls ip binding** command. In addition to triggering the generation of labels, the **mpls ip** command also starts the label distribution protocol (LDP) and the search for LDP peers. The current version of LDP only supports IPv4 and uses IPv4 to form relationships. The routers will start send multicast LDP hellos as probes to 224.0.0.2 to UDP port 646 to try and discover another LDP router. The source of the packets will be based on the LDP router ID. Which, like other protocols, if not statically configured, will be based on a Loopback interface with the largest numeric value. Unlike the other protocols with a router ID, the router ID for LDP needs to be reachable. The LDP peer relationship is formed between the router IDs. If a neighbor is found, than the two will form a TCP session between the router IDs using the TCP port number 646.

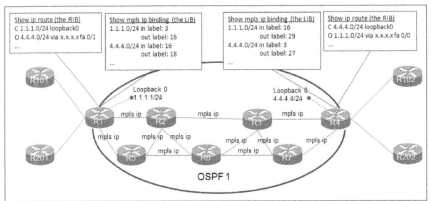

At this point the LDP neighbors will start to distribute labels for the routes within their RIB. The Cisco routers do what referred to as liberal retention, which means that all labels heard from a peer will be kept within the LIB, even from peers that are not in the forwarding path. The only labels that a LDP peer will not keep are labels related to a route that the receiving router doesn't have in it RIB. Now looking at the LIB, you'll see that there are local labels (in) and remote labels (out) learned from its peer. The point of liberal retention is so that if there is a path change (such as the interface between R1 and R2 fails and OSPF converges to forward through R5), MPLS will not contribute to the time for convergence. The labels are already known from all peers, so once OSPF stabilizes and the FIB is repopulated, the LFIB will pull from the LIB the label for the new path. No additional LDP distribution is needed.

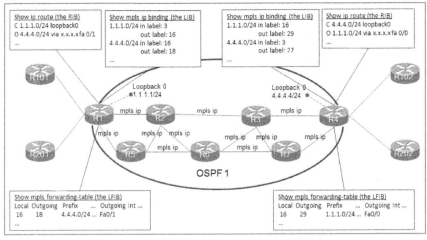

The router then compares the Forwarding Information Base (FIB) for the path that is considered to be best and looks within the LIB to see if there is a corresponding remote or out label. If so, then it populate the Label Forwarding Information Base (LFIB) with the label information for every prefix. The local label or in label will be linked to the remote or out label. So, if the router receives a labeled packet, then the router will swap the label based on the LFIB. If the inbound packet doesn't have a label, then the router uses the FIB for forwarding. There are hooks to the LFIB, so that if there is a corresponding out label, the router will impose a label and send it out to the next router within the path. If the router receives a packet with a label that it doesn't find an entry in the LFIB, the router will pop the label and try to forward the packet based on the IPv4 forwarding table. To see the LFIB, use the **show mpls forwarding-table** command. In this example, R1 has a local label of 16 for the 4.4.4.0/24 route and an outgoing label of 18 that it learned from its LDP peer, R2. The LIB would also contain labels from R5, but since R5 is not in the primary path, it does not show up in the LFIB. If R1 receives a packet with an MPLS header with a label 16, it will swap it to 18 and send in out to R2. If R1 receives an IPv4 packet distended to 4.4.4.0/24, then R1 will impose a label of 18 and send it to R2...this includes traffic originating on R1.

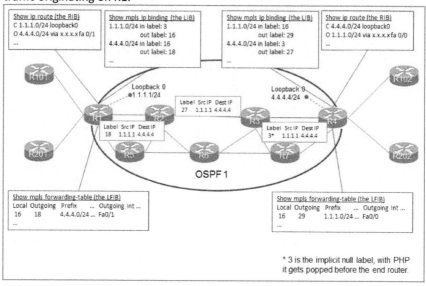

The previous and following images show the label swapping is a packet is sent from R1 to R4's Loopback, sourced from R1's loopback (such as a ping). The assumption is that the process of passing labels have already been completed between all routers within the core network. R1 imposes a label of 18 and send the packet out to R2. R2 looks up the label in the LFIB and sees that it has pulled a label of 27 from the LIB that it learned from R3. R2 replaces or swaps the label 18 with the label 27 and sends it to R3. When R3 receives the labeled packet, it looks up the label 27 and sees there is an outgoing label of 3 that it learned from R4. Label 3 is a special meaning label, the implicit null label. Cisco (and others) do penultimate hop popping (PHP), which is that the next to last (penultimate) router will pop the label. This is still considered to be label swapping since the lookup is based on the LFIB, not based on the IPv4 header. PHP is the default behavior for the Cisco routers and all routes that are injected by a router will be labeled with a label of 3. This would be true for routes being injected from outside the MPLS core as well as routes redistributed into the core IGP.

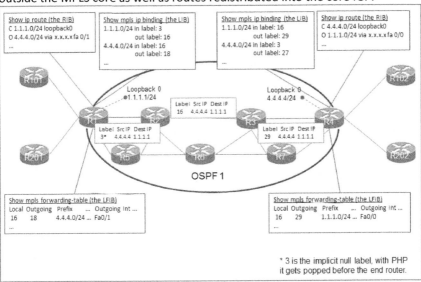

The process is the same in the reverse direction. The label switch path (LSP) is unidirectional, meaning that the return path does not have to follow the forward path. In this example it does, but it doesn't have to. If PBR or static routes were used to dictate the forwarding path, the LSP will follow that same path. The exception to this would be MPLS traffic engineering (MPLS TE) that uses constraints based routing, but that is beyond the scope of this course since it is not on the CCIE R&S practical exam version 5.0 blueprint.

So what's the point of all this? Yes, we are using labels to make forwarding decisions, but all routers still have complete IPv4 forwarding tables. All the core routers have the same size routing tables, no saving. When this will first thought of, the saving was the processing time for looking up labels versus looking IPv4 destinations. Now that most routers do forwarding within hardware, there is not much benefit to forwarding based on labels rather than based on layer 3 addressing.

The next step was to look for another application for MPLS that would be a bit more useful. If we look at the provider space, we had an issue with BGP passing routing information through the core of the network.

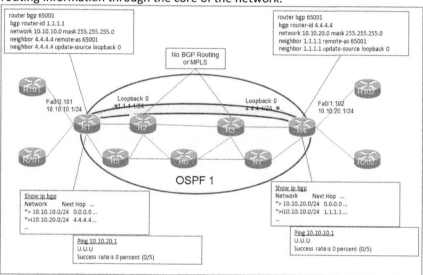

Having the edge router be BGP speakers peering to each other, allowed the routing information of the outside routers to be passed, but the issue is that there are routers that in the path that are not BGP speakers. If the edge router just accepted the routes without question, the RIB/FIB of R1 and R4 would be complete, but the traffic would fail. In this example, R1 is pinging an address that is beyond R4 that it learned through BGP. When R1 goes to forward the packet, it is determined that there is no outgoing interface for the destination. At which point, R1 will have to do a second (recursive) lookup on how to get to the source of the route (R4). It then determines that the path is to R2 to get to R4. When the packet gets to R2, there is no route to the destination, therefore the packet is dropped. Cisco had synchronization enabled for quite a while to force up to resolve the issue. There are several solutions to this problem: turn on BGP on all the routers; redistribute BGP into the IGPs; tunnel the BGP process between R1 and R4 (forming the BGP session through a GRE tunnel). If we think of MPLS as a tunneling protocol, that could be used to help the BGP issues. Extensions were written to BGP to generate additional labels for the routes that BGP propagates. This means that LDP does not generate labels for BGP routes, all other, but BGP.

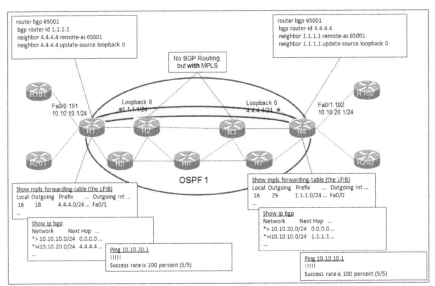

Adding MPLS into the mix, BGP will generate its own set of labels that are "piggybacked" with the route update, as defined in RFC 3107. The LDP labels will still be generated based of off the RIB (all routes, except BGP learned routes) and will therefore be used to help the BGP speakers reach each other. When BGP recognizes that the path between speakers is a label switch path, then BGP will generate its own set of labels, one for each route within the BGP table and pass that to the other BGP speaker. Notice in the diagram, there are no new commands to make this happen. It is solely based on the fact that the path between peers is a LSP. Now the intermediate routers will pass the traffic based on a label, not based on IPv4 forwarding. The edge routers will impose a label stack. The outer label is the LDP learned label, used to reach the loopback of the other BGP speaker. The inside label is the BGP label and is only meaningful to the other BGP speaker. If an intermediate router was to pop the outside label prematurely, the router would then see the inside label, but not have an entry in its LFIB, therefore not know what to do with that label. It would pop again to expose the underlying IPv4 header and then try to forward it based on the destination IPv4 address. It is most likely that it wouldn't have a route, so unless the router had a default route, the packet would be dropped.

This combination of BGP and MPLS turns out to be very helpful. The intermediate routers don't have to have BGP running and they also don't have to have complete routing tables. In this case, MPLS is used to "hide" the BGP routes and any traffic that is associated with those routes. Before MPLS, either all routers would have to be BGP speakers, or redistribution between BGP and the IGP (synchronization would most likely be used) or a tunnel could be used between the BGP speakers. The first two options doesn't scale well, so a lot of providers used the third option...GRE between edge routers, peering BGP through the tunnel, therefore hiding the routes and traffic from the intermediate routers. So, you could make an argument that MPLS is a type of tunneling protocol...and I would have to agree. In my mind, if you are encapsulating something within something else, you're tunneling. This was the first "killer app" for MPLS in the provider space. We could use it to get rid of a lot of GRE tunnels. The natural extension to this was to carrier customer routes and traffic through MPLS, via BGP, but keep them separate...VPNs!

Implement Layer 3 virtual private networks (VPNs) on provider edge (PE), provider (P), and customer edge (CE) routers

Now that we've seen a usable application of MPLS with BGP, and what I could consider what would satisfy the first part of the version 5.0 of the blueprint relative to MPLS. We will continue to look at the next significant application of MPLS, layer 3 VPNs. First let's look at the components needed to support MPLS Layer 3 VPNs through the core network. First is BGP, which we just got done looking at. The second are virtual routing and forwarding tables (VRF). Let do a review of VRFs.

Implement virtual routing and forwarding (VRF) and Multi-VRF Customer Edge (VRF-Lite)

Virtual Routing and Forwarding (VRF) is an IP technology that allows multiple instances of a routing table to coexist on the same router at the same time. Because the routing instances are independent, the same or overlapping IP addresses can be used without conflict. "VRF" is also used to refer to a routing table instance that can exist in one or multiple instances per each VPN on a Provider Edge (PE) router (which will get to shortly). VRF-Lite is an application where there is no MPLS functionality on the router.

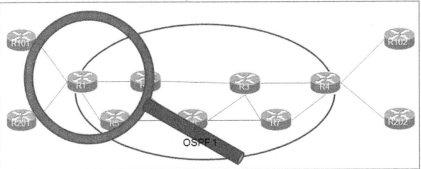

If we look at one of the routers and pull it out of the network of a minute, we can look at an example of an implementation of VRF lite.

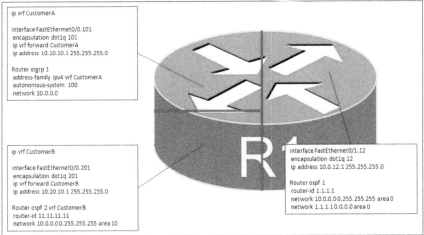

```
ip vrf CustomerA

interface FastEthernet0/0.101
 encapsulation dot1q 101
 ip vrf forward CustomerA
 ip address 10.10.10.1 255.255.255.0

Router eigrp 1
 address-family ipv4 vrf CustomerA
 autonomous-system 100
 network 10.0.0.0
```

```
ip vrf CustomerB

interface FastEthernet0/0.201
 encapsulation dot1q 201
 ip vrf forward CustomerB
 ip address 10.20.10.1 255.255.255.0

Router ospf 2 vrf CustomerB
 router-id 11.11.11.11
 network 10.0.0.0 0.255.255.255 area 10
```

```
interface FastEthernet0/1.12
 encapsulation dot1q 12
 ip address 10.0.12.1 255.255.255.0

Router ospf 1
 router-id 1.1.1.1
 network 10.0.0.0 0.255.255.255 area 0
 network 1.1.1.1 0.0.0.0 area 0
```

With VRF lite, there is no need for a route distinguisher or route target, the VRFs are standalone and are locally significant. Each definition creates a different routing context that can support different routing protocols. The **ip vrf** command still works, but to make the vrf more generic, use the **vrf definition** command instead. Under the vrf definition you can apply different address families if needed and will support both IPv4 and IPv6.

To move an interface from the global routing table to a vrf table, use the **ip vrf forward** or **vrf forward** command at the interface level. If there are preconfigured address on the interface, they will be removed once the vrf command is issued at the interface level.

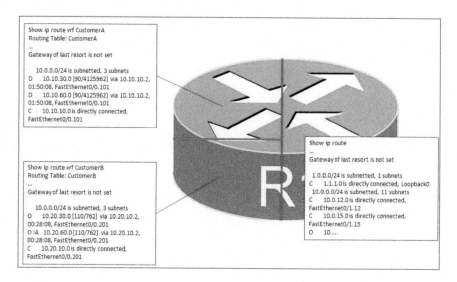

MPLS Layer 3 VPNs

Per Cisco, MPLS Layer 3 VPNs use a peer-to-peer model that uses Border Gateway Protocol (BGP) to distribute VPN-related information. Service providers can then offer value-added services like Quality of Service (QoS) and Traffic Engineering, allowing network convergence that encompasses voice, video, and data. The Layer 3 VPN over Multiprotocol Label Switching (MPLS) is the most widely deployed MPLS application in Service Provider and self-managed Enterprise networks. The Cisco IOS Software implementation of this architecture (RFC 2547, later updated by 4364) provides secure control and forwarding planes upon which to build robust VPNs.

Virtual Routing Forwarding instances constructed by Multiprotocol-Border Gateway Protocol (MP-BGP) provide adequate routing separation on a shared multi-service edge. The integration between MP-BGP and MPLS technology allows users to maintain separation between traffic from multiple subscriber networks as the traffic is switched through a single shared core.

Cisco IOS MPLS Layer 3 VPNs enable Service Providers to offer any-to-any connectivity services that can be implemented over either an MPLS or an IP infrastructure.

To meet unique customer requirements, Cisco has also extended MPLS Layer3 VPN support over IP with MPLS VPN over IP. This solution, which supports Layer 3 VPNs for L2TPv3, eliminates the need to implement MPLS in the core.

So, that's great, but what does that mean to me (or you)? We can extend a customer from one site to another, through an MPLS cloud using BGP and keep them separate.

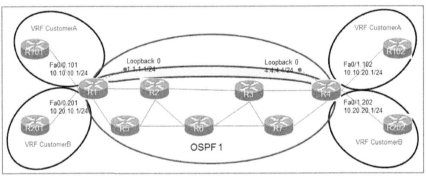

At this point, we need to combine a few features together...MPLS, BGP and VRFs. The VRFs need to be modified from VRF lite.

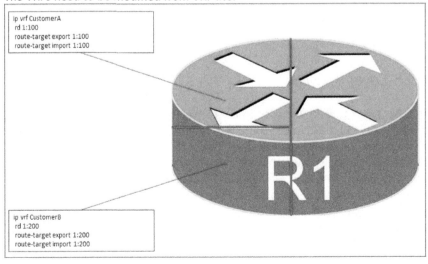

First we need something to help if we have overlapping addressing from our customers. Route Distinguisher! As its name implies, a route distinguisher (RD) DISTINGUISHES one set of routes (one VRF) from another. It is a unique number prepended to each route within a VRF to identify it as belonging to that particular VRF or customer. An RD is carried along with a route via MP-BGP when exchanging VPN routes with other PE routers. An RD is 64 bits in length comprising three fields: type (two bytes), administrator, and value. There are three types:

- Type 0: 2 byte ASN field and 4 byte value
- Type 1: 4 byte IP and 2 byte value
- Type 2: 5 byte ASN field and 2 byte value

The choice of format is largely cosmetic: It makes no difference to BGP as the RD is effectively just a flat number prepended to a route. The choice of formats exists solely to allow for flexible administration of the number space.
When VPN routes are advertised among PE routers via MP-BGP, the RD is included as part of the route along with the IP prefix and is sent as an extended community string.
Route distinguishers are used to maintain uniqueness among identical routes in different VRFs, and initially, that was good enough for extending a VRF from edge router to edge router. It was determined fairly quickly that addition functionality was desired, such as leaking routes from one VRF to another for features like shared services or managed services. Route targets can be used to share routes among those VRFs. We can apply route targets to a VRF to control the import and export of routes with it and between other VRFs.
A route target takes the form of an extended BGP community with a structure similar to that of a route distinguisher (which is probably why the two are so easily confused).

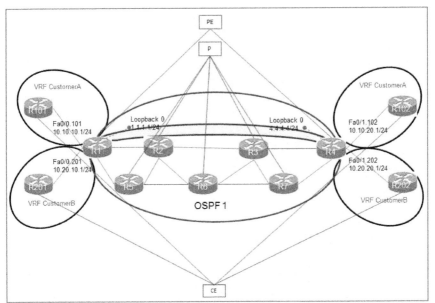

At this point it's helpful to define the roles of the routers involved with this topology:

- Provider Edge (PE): routers which are at the edge of the MPLS cloud and are the BGP speakers peering to other PE routers and are visible at layer 3 to the customer.

- Provider Core (P): core routers that are forwarding from PE to PE using labels. Typically are not BGP speakers (some use P routers as route reflectors), but are participating in the core IGP.

- Customer Edge (CE): customer router interfacing with the PE router, but not running MPLS (typically). May be configured with a default route pointing to the PE router; running an IGP to the PE router; or running BGP and peering to the PE router.

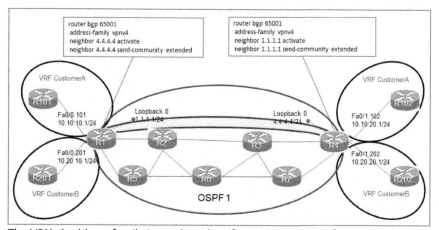

The VPNv4 address family is used to identify routing sessions for protocols such as BGP that use standard VPN Version 4 address prefixes. Unicast address prefixes are the default when VPNv4 address prefixes are configured. VPNv4 routes are the same as IPv4 routes, but VPNv4 routes have a route descriptor (RD) prepended that allows replication of prefixes. It is possible to associate every different RD with a different VPN. Each VPN needs its own set of prefixes. Activating a neighbor under the address family VPNV4 now enables the potential of passing VPNv4 routes to that neighbor. Note the addition of the **send-community extended** for that neighbor as well. Since the RD and possible RT are sent as extended community strings, you have to allow the router to send those strings. As discussed in the **Stupid CCIE Tricks - section 7: BGP**, community strings are optional transitive attributes, but are not sent by default, therefore you have to grant the router "permission" to send the communities. This configuration will cause the neighbors to reset, since this is a change in capabilities and that is only sent in the Open message at the initialization of the peering session.

At this point, nothing new is really happening, other than the neighbors are capable of extending a VRF through a VPN to each other.

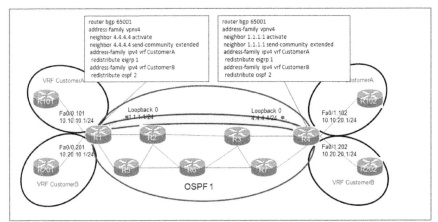

To extend the VRF, the address family IPv4 VRF is used under BGP to configure what is to be advertised between the BGP speakers. You can use network statements, redistribution or neighbor statements to the CE router to inject routes into the BGP process for this VRF. Once this is done, the routes should be passed between the PE routers. You can use the **show ip bgp vpnv4 all** command to see the different VRF tables that are populated by BGP.

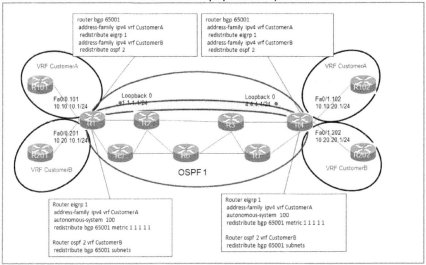

Now that the routes on the PE router, you need to get them to the CE routers. If the CE routers are using default routes to the PE, then you're done. If an IGP is used between the PE and CE routers, then we need to redistribute BGP into the IGP. With RIP and EIGRP, the redistribution is done under the address family for the VRF in the RIP or EIGRP routing process. For OSPF, it would be done under the routing context for the specific VRF. With RIP and EIGRP, there is still a requirement for a seed metric to get the routes advertised, but the seed is not used if the remote IGP is the same as the local between the PE and CE routers.

If BGP is running between the CE and PE routers, we need to modify the routes so they will be accepted by the CE. On the PE router, you'll need to add an extra neighbor statement of **neighbor as-override**. This will replace the customers' ASN with the PE ASN so the CE router doesn't reject the route from the PE router.

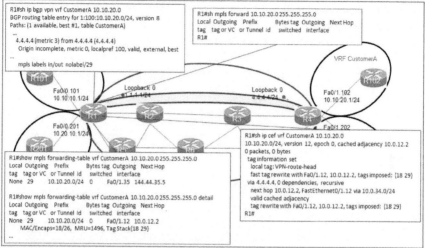

Now that we have the routes in the BGP table for the VRF, we get a bit more detail when we look at the specific route. Notice that there is an outgoing label of 29 listed in the BGP table. This is the label that the other PE router advertised to R1 in this case. If you look for that route in the LFIB with the **show mpls forwarding-table** command, the route is not in the table. Why? Because we're looking at the LFIB as it relates to the global routing table, not the VRF. If you look at the route relative to the VRF, then we get output about that route. Again, notice that the label is the same from BGP. If we add the keyword **detail**, then we see that there is a label stack that is imposed. If you look at IP CEF relative to the VRF and that route, again we see the label stack that is imposed to send traffic to that subnet.

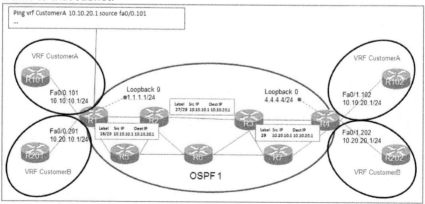

Now when we pass traffic from R1 (PE) to r4 (PE) using the VRF, there is a label stack used to provide reachability. The outside label from R1 in this case is 18; R2 knows and switches to 27 that it learned from R3; R3 knows 27 and has the pop label from R4, so it pops the outside label. R1 had also imposed an inside label of 29 that it learned from R4 for that specific route. When R3 pops the outside label since Cisco does PHP by default and it exposes the inside label. At this point R3 had already done its lookup and send the packet out without looking up the 29. R4 knows of 29 as a BGP route in VRF CustomerA. It then follows the VRF to forward the traffic to the proper interface, which in this case is its own address.

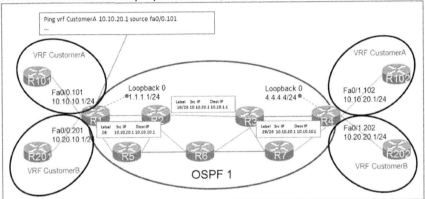

The return follows the exact same process.

Modification to the Normal Redistribution Rules

Redistribution of OSPF into BGP

When redistributing OSPF into another protocol, the normal process is to pass all OSPF routes (Internal, External type 1 and External type 2). This is normally true, even if the target protocol is BGP. In the case of BGP being used to extend a layer 3 VPN, the behavior is modified. When redistributing OSPF into BGP, when BGP is involved with a layer 3 VPN, then on Internal routes will be passed. The assumption is that BGP may have been redistributed into OSPF, therefore passing the external routes may cause a routing loop. To get OSPF to pass the external routes, just use the **match** option on the redistribute command line (ex.: *redistribute ospf 1 match internal external 1 external 2*).

Redistribution of BGP into the IGP

Normally with BGP, when you redistribute BGP into an IGP, it would be considered undesirable to pass iBGP learned routes into an IGP. The concern is that if you were configured for synchronization and you have already redistribute the IGP into BGP, this could cause a routing loop. So, as stated in the **Stupid CCIE Tricks v5.0 - section 7: BGP**, when you redistribute BGP into an IGP, only eBGP learned routes would be passed. With MPLS Layer 3 VPNs, that would defeat the purpose of the process. Normally to get the iBGP learned routes to be passed, you would have to go under the BGP process and add the **bgp redistribute internal** command. This is not necessary in this case. It is understood with the VPN operations, there is a need to pass the iBGP learned routes, since that is the most likely source of routers from the other PE.

EGIRP and OSPF External or Native

Again, normally if you redistribute anything into EIGRP or OSPF, the default behavior would be to mark those routes as external. But in the case of a Layer 3 VPN, that could have a negative effect. In general, we are trying to hide the provider network. So, extensions were added to BGP to propagate information about the source IGP. Cisco has added additional extension to support EIGRP. In both cases, if the original IGP and target IGP are the same and the configuration is consistent, then the routes will be seen as native to the target protocol. EIGRP will have its original composite metrics, even though you do have to configure metrics for the redistribution to work.

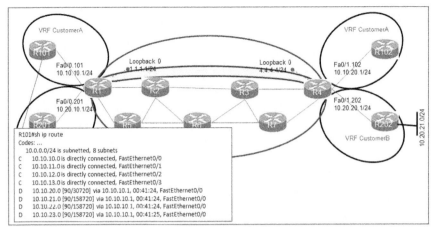

OSPF will be inter-area (LSA type 3) routes, only if the PE routers are configured with the same domain identifier. We will talk about sham links shortly, if you need the routes to be sent as intra-area (LSA type 1 for OSPFv2) routes.

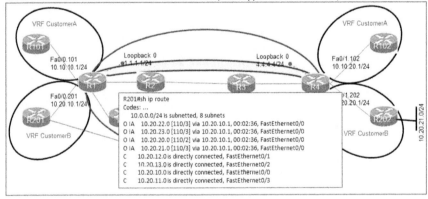

Advanced Options

Sham Links

Although OSPF PE-CE connections assume that the only path between two client sites is across the MPLS VPN backbone, backdoor paths between VPN sites may exist. If these sites belong to the same OSPF area, the path over a backdoor link will always be selected because OSPF prefers intra-area (LSA 1) paths to inter-area (LSA 3) paths over the MPLS links. PE routers advertise OSPF routes learned over the VPN backbone as either external routes or inter-area routes, dependent on the domain ID of the PE routers. For this reason, OSPF backdoor links between VPN sites must be taken into account so that routing will take the contracted MPLS path.

Here we have an example of a backdoor path over the Frame Relay cloud.

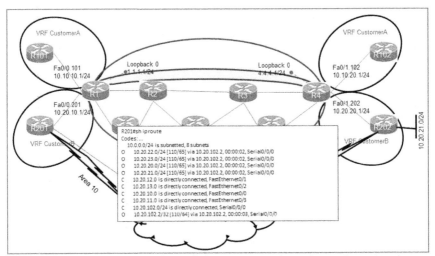

As you can see, the routing tables of the CE routes show the preferred path over the Frame Relay link, not towards the PE router.

To reestablish the desired path selection over the MPLS VPN backbone, you must create an additional OSPF intra-area (logical) link between ingress and egress VRFs on the relevant PE routers. This link is called a sham-link.

A sham-link is required between any two VPN sites that belong to the same OSPF area and share an OSPF backdoor link. If no backdoor link exists between the sites, no sham-link is required.

When a sham-link is configured between PE routers, the PEs can populate the VRF routing table with the OSPF routes learned over the sham-link.

Before you create a sham-link between PE routers in an MPLS VPN, you must:

- Configure a separate /32 address on the PE routers so that OSPF packets can be sent over the VPN backbone to the remote end of the sham-link. The /32 address must meet the following criteria:
    - Belong to the VRF of the customer with a backdoor
    - You should not advertised the new /32 by OSPF
    - Be advertised by BGP in the VRF with the backdoor

Associate the sham-link with an existing OSPF area.

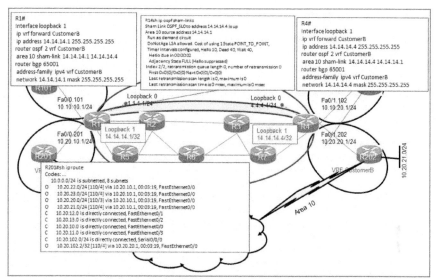

So, in this example, I've added a Loopback 1 on the two PE routers. The interfaces are part of the VRF being extended that the Frame Relay link is the backdoor to. Add a network statement under the address family for that VRF, under BGP. Added under the OSPF routing process for the VRF the **area 10 sham-link** command with the local address, then the remote PE address. Use the **show ip ospf sham-link** command to determine the state of the sham link. Link the **show ip ospf virtual-link** command, there are two parts to the output of the show command. The top portion that shows that the sham link is up, just indicates that the sham link is configured and the target addresses in the **area sham-link** command are known in that VRF. The lower portion shows the adjacency with the other PE router, which needs to be in a **full** state, otherwise your sham link isn't really up.

We can now see from the CE router's routing table that the preferred path is through the PE router.

Static MPLS Label Assignment

Generally, label switching routers (LSRs) dynamically learn the labels they should use to label-switch packets by means of label distribution protocols that include:

- Label Distribution Protocol (LDP), the Internet Engineering Task Force (IETF) standard, used to bind labels to network addresses

- Resource Reservation Protocol (RSVP) used to distribute labels for traffic engineering (TE)

- Border Gateway Protocol (BGP) used to distribute labels for Multiprotocol Label Switching (MPLS) Virtual Private Networks (VPNs)

To use a learned label to label-switch packets, an LSR installs the label into its Label Forwarding Information Base (LFIB).
The MPLS Static Labels feature provides the means to configure statically:
- The binding between a label and an IPv4 prefix
- The contents of an LFIB cross connect entry

Static bindings between labels and IPv4 prefixes can be configured to support MPLS hop-by-hop forwarding, even if LDP is not being used. To configure MPLS static prefix/label bindings, use the following commands beginning in global configuration mode:

```
Router(config)# mpls label range min-label max-label [static min-static-label max-static-label]
```

	— Default is no labels reserved for static assignment	
minimum-value	The value of the smallest label allowed in the label space. The default is 16.	
maximum-value	The value of the largest label allowed in the label space. The default is platform-dependent.	
static	(Optional) Reserves a block of local labels for static label assignments. If you omit the static keyword and the minimum-static-value maximum-static-value arguments, no labels are reserved for static assignment.	
minimum-static-value	(Optional) The minimum value for static label assignments. There is no default value.	
maximum-static-value	(Optional) The maximum value for static label assignments. There is no default value.	

```
Router(config)# mpls static binding ipv4 prefix mask [input | output nexthop] label
```

	— Bindings specified are installed automatically in the MPLS forwarding table as routing demands.	
prefix mask	Specifies the prefix and mask to bind to a label. (When you do not use the input or output keyword, the specified label is an incoming label.)	
	Note	Without the arguments, the no form of the command removes all static bindings.
label	Binds a prefix or a mask to a local (incoming) label. (When you do not use the input or output keyword, the specified	

	label is an incoming label.)
input *label*	Binds the specified label to the prefix and mask as a local (incoming) label.
output *nexthop* explicit-null	Binds the Internet Engineering Task Force (IETF) Multiprotocol Label Switching (MPLS) IPv4 explicit null label (0) as a remote (outgoing) label.
output *nexthop* implicit-null	Binds the IETF MPLS implicit null label (3) as a remote (outgoing) label.
output nexthop label	Binds the specified label to the prefix/mask as a remote (outgoing) label.

Use the **show mpls label range** command to see how many labels are set aside for static mapping. Use the **show mpls static binding ipv4** command to verify the static prefix to label bindings.

MPLS LDP Authentication

The MPLS LDP—Lossless MD5 Session Authentication feature enables a Label Distribution Protocol (LDP) session to be password-protected without tearing down and reestablishing the LDP session. To configure a message digest algorithm 5 (MD5) password for Label Distribution Protocol (LDP) sessions with neighbors whose LDP router IDs are permitted by a specified access list, use the **mpls ldp password option** command in global configuration mode.

```
Router(config)# mpls ldp [ vrf vrf-name ] password option number
for acl { key-chain keychain-name | [ 0 | 7 ] } password
```

vrf vrf-name	(Optional) Specifies a VPN routing and forwarding (VRF) instance configured on the label switch router (LSR).
number	The option number. A comparison of the number argument from several commands by the software sets up the order in which LDP evaluates access lists in the definition of a password for the neighbor. The valid range is from 1 to 32767.
for *acl*	Specifies the name of the access list that includes the LDP router IDs of those neighbors for which the password applies. Only standard IP access lists can be used for the acl argument.
key-chain keychain-	Specifies the name of the key chain used to specify the MD5 key that authenticates the exchange of bidirectional

name	LDP traffic.
0	(Optional) Specifies that the password is an unencrypted password.
7	(Optional) Specifies that the password is an encrypted password.
password	Specifies the MD5 password to be used for the specified LDP sessions.

The following is an example of how to configure authentication for MPLS:

```
key chain MyKey
key 1
key-string cisco
send-lifetime 10:00:00 Nov 2 2013 10:00:00 Dec 2 2013
accept-lifetime 00:00:00 Jan 1 1970 duration 1
key 2
key-string cisco2
send-lifetime 00:00:00 Jan 1 1970 duration 1
accept-lifetime 10:00:00 Nov 2 2013 10:00:00 Nov 17 2013
!
mpls ldp password option 1 for nbr-acl key-chain MyKey
```

Disabling Penultimate Hop Popping

How do you disable PHP? Well, you really can't, but... Have the egress router send an explicit null, rather than the implicit null label!

The MPLS Label Stack Encoding standard (RFC 3032) specifies two reserved values (among others) that are useful in the last hop of a Label Switched Path (LSP):

- 0: explicit NULL. Can be used in signaling protocols as well as label headers.

- 3: implicit NULL. Used in signaling protocols only. It should never appear in the label stack. Its use in a signaling protocol indicates that the upstream router should perform *penultimate hop popping* (PHP; remove the top label on the stack).

The implicit NULL should be used whenever possible, as the PHP reduces the amount of lookup required on the last hop of an LSP (sometimes that could mean the difference between hardware and software lookup). Implicit nulls are automatically popped, explicit nulls are not!

```
R1(config)# mpls ldp explicit-null [ for prefix-acl | to peer-
acl | for prefix-acl to peer-acl ]
```

for prefix-acl	(Optional) Specifies prefixes for which Explicit Null should be advertised in place of Implicit Null.
to peer-acl	(Optional) Specifies Label Distribution Protocol (LDP) peers to which Explicit Null should be advertised in place of Implicit Null.

Conditional Label Advertisement

MPLS LDP Conditional Label Advertisement enables the ability to advertise labels for a certain FECs to a selected group of LDP peers. To control the distribution of locally assigned (incoming) labels by means of label distribution protocol (LDP), use the **mpls ldp advertise-labels** command in global configuration mode.

```
Router(config)# [no] mpls ldp advertise-labels [ vrf vrf-name ] [
interface interface | for prefix-access-list [ to peer-
access-list ] ]
```

vrf vrf-name	(Optional) Specifies the Virtual Private Network (VPN) routing and forwarding (VFR) instance for label advertisement.
interface *interface*	(Optional) Specifies an interface for label advertisement of an interface address.
for prefix-access-list	(Optional) Specifies which destinations should have their labels advertised.
to peer-access-list	(Optional) Specifies which LDP neighbors should receive label advertisements. An LSR is identified by its router ID, which consists of the first 4 bytes of its 6-byte LDP identifier.

The following is an example of how to configure conditional label advertisement:

```
access-list 1 per 1.1.1.0 0.0.0.0
access-list 2 per 192.168.12.2 0.0.0.0
!
no mpls ldp advertise-labels
mpls ldp advertise-labels for 1 to 2
```

Route Leaking Between VRFs

Sometimes there's a need to have routes from one VRF show up in another or from the global routing table in a VRF table. This is referred to as route leaking. We'll look at both possibilities. First let's look at leaking between the global routing table and a VRF.

```
ip vrf vpn1
rd 100:1
route-target export 100:1
route-target import 100:1
!
interface Serial1/0
 ip address 10.1.2.1 255.255.255.252
 no ip directed-broadcast
!
interface Serial1/1
 ip vrf forwarding vpn1
 ip address 10.0.2.1 255.255.255.0
 no ip directed-broadcast
!
ip classless
ip route 10.0.2.0 255.255.255.252 Serial2/0
ip route vrf vpn2 10.1.2.4 255.255.255.252 10.1.2.2 global
!
```

In the preceding example, there a couple static routes. The first is injecting a route into the global routing table for the network that is on interface serial 1/1, which is part of VRF vpn1. The second static route injects a route into the VRF table for vpn1, but the next hop is found in the global routing table. The keyword **global** identifies the next hop is from the global routing table. As an alternative, we could have point the second static route out serial 1/0.

To leak between VRFs, there are options. We can leak with or without route maps. The direction of the leaking indicates the type of map, either import map or export map. Let's first look at it with any route map. We simply have to add the route target exported from one VRF as an import of another. Notice this can be done on the same router or could be on others.

```
ip vrf vpn1
 rd 100:1
 route-target export 100:1
 route-target import 100:1
 route-target import 200:1
!
ip vrf vpn2
 rd 200:1
 route-target export 200:1
 route-target import 200:1
 route-target import 100:1
```

Now let's look at it with an export map. With the export map, we use a route map to define which routes will get a new route target to be exported with. The route map will call an access list or prefix list to define those routes. Route targets are sent as extended communities in BGP, so we have to set the excommunity with the addition keyword of **rt** to indicate that this is a route target. The keyword **additive** is need so that the original route target will still be sent. The VRF that is to import the routes will have the new import route target.

```
ip vrf vpn1
 rd 100:1
 route-target both 100:1
 route-target import 17:17
!
```

```
ip                         vrf                              vpn2
 rd                                                         200:1
 export                         map                       2Routes
 route-target                    both                       200:1
 !
access-list            1              permit              1.2.3.0
access-list            1              permit              2.3.4.0
 !
route-map              2Routes                permit            10
 match                  ip                 address             1
 set extcommunity rt 17:17 additive
```

With an import map, it effects all routes being imported into this VRF, so the route map has to match on the "normal" route target as well as the route target you want to control. This requires a couple extended community lists to match on those route targets. We also need an access list or prefix list to define the routes we want to import. The route map then matches on those extended community lists and access/prefix list to allow those to be imported.

```
ip vrf vpn1
 rd 100:1
 route-target both 100:1
 import map AllRoutes
 !
ip                         vrf                              vpn2
 rd                                                         200:1
 route-target                    both                       200:1
 !
access-list            1              permit              1.2.3.0
access-list            1              permit              2.3.4.0
 !
ip extcommunity-list standard VPN1 permit rt 100:1
ip extcommunity-list standard VPN2 permit rt 200:1
 !
route-map AllRoutes permit 10
 match extcommunity VPN1
 !
route-map              AllRoutes              permit            20
 match                  ip                 address             1
 match extcommunity VPN2
```

One Label per VRF

By default, Cisco routers generate a label per entry in the VRF and BGP table(s). This can be overwhelming for a receiving router or you may just run out of labels. To configure per virtual routing and forwarding (VRF) labels, use the **mpls label mode** command in global configuration mode.

```
R1(config)# mpls label mode { vrf vrf-name | all-vrfs } protocol
bgp-vpnv4 { per-prefix | per-vrf | vrf-conn-aggr }
```

vrf	Configures a single VPN routing and forwarding (VRF) domain.
vrf-name	Name for the single VRF to configure.
all-vrfs	Configures a label mode for all VRFs on the router.
protocol	Specifies a protocol to use for the label mode.
bgp-vpnv4	Specifies the IPv4 VRF address-family protocol for the label mode configuration.
per-prefix	Specifies per-prefix label mode.
per-vrf	Specifies per-VRF label mode.
vrf-conn-aggr	Specifies per-VRF label mode for connected and Border Gateway Protocol (BGP) aggregates in the VRF.

Configuration Commands

The following are some of the more common commands used in configuring and supporting MPLS, based on the CCIE Routing & Switching version 5.0 blueprint.

clear mpls ldp neighbor

To forcibly reset a label distribution protocol (LDP) session, use the **clear mpls ldp neighbor** command in privileged EXEC mode.

```
clear mpls ldp neighbor [ vrf vrf-name ] { nbr-address | * }
```

vrf vrf-name	(Optional) Specifies the VPN routing and forwarding instance (vrf-name) for resetting an LDP session.
nbr-address	Specifies the address of the LDP neighbor whose session will be reset. The neighbor address is treated as <nbr-address>:0, which means it pertains to the LDP session for the LSR's platform-wide label space.
*	Designates that all LDP sessions will be reset.

mpls ip (interface configuration)

To enable Multiprotocol Label Switching (MPLS) forwarding of IPv4 packets along normally routed paths for a particular interface, use the **mpls ip** command in interface configuration mode.

```
mpls ip
```

mpls ip default-route

To enable the distribution of labels associated with the IP default route, use the **mpls ip default-route** command in global configuration mode.

```
mpls ip default-route
```

mpls ip propagate-ttl

To control the generation of the time-to-live (TTL) field in the Multiprotocol Label Switching (MPLS) header when labels are first added to an IP packet, use the **mpls ip propagate-ttl** command in global configuration mode. To use a fixed TTL value (255) for the first label of the IP packet, use the **no** form of this command.

```
mpls ip propagate-ttl
no mpls ip propagate-ttl [ forwarded | local ]
```

| forwarded | (Optional) Prevents the traceroute command from showing the hops for forwarded packets. |
| local | (Optional) Prevents the traceroute command from showing the hops only for local packets. |

This command is enabled by default. The TTL field is copied from the IP header. A traceroute command shows all of the hops in the network.

mpls label mode

To configure per virtual routing and forwarding (VRF) labels, use the **mpls label mode** command in global configuration mode.

```
mpls label mode { vrf vrf-name | all-vrfs } protocol bgp-vpnv4 {
per-prefix | per-vrf | vrf-conn-aggr }
```

vrf	Configures a single VPN routing and forwarding (VRF) domain.
vrf-name	Name for the single VRF to configure.
all-vrfs	Configures a label mode for all VRFs on the router.
protocol	Specifies a protocol to use for the label mode.
bgp-vpnv4	Specifies the IPv4 VRF address-family protocol for the label mode configuration.
per-prefix	Specifies per-prefix label mode.
per-vrf	Specifies per-VRF label mode.
vrf-conn-aggr	Specifies per-VRF label mode for connected and Border Gateway Protocol (BGP) aggregates in the VRF.

Per-prefix label mode is the default.

mpls label range

To configure the range of local labels available for use with Multiprotocol Label Switching (MPLS) applications on packet interfaces, use the **mpls label range** command in global configuration mode.

```
mpls label range minimum-value maximum-value [ static minimum-
static-value maximum-static-value ]
```

minimum-value	The value of the smallest label allowed in the label space. The default is 16.
maximum-value	The value of the largest label allowed in the label space. The default is platform-dependent.
static	(Optional) Reserves a block of local labels for static label assignments. If you omit the static keyword and the minimum-static-value maximum-static-value arguments, no labels are reserved for static assignment.
minimum-static-value	(Optional) The minimum value for static label assignments. There is no default value.
maximum-static-value	(Optional) The maximum value for static label assignments. There is no default value.

mpls ldp advertise-labels

To control the distribution of locally assigned (incoming) labels by means of label distribution protocol (LDP), use the **mpls ldp advertise-labels** command in global configuration mode.

```
mpls ldp advertise-labels [ vrf vrf-name ] [ interface interface |
for prefix-access-list [ to peer-access-list ] ]
```

vrf vrf-name	(Optional) Specifies the Virtual Private Network (VPN) routing and forwarding (VFR) instance for label advertisement.
interface *interface*	(Optional) Specifies an interface for label advertisement of an interface address.
for prefix-access-list	(Optional) Specifies which destinations should have their labels advertised.
to peer-access-list	(Optional) Specifies which LDP neighbors should receive label advertisements. An LSR is identified by its router ID, which consists of the first 4 bytes of its 6-byte LDP identifier.

The labels of all destinations are advertised to all LDP neighbors. If the vrf keyword is not specified, this command applies to the default routing domain. If the interface keyword is not specified, no label is advertised for the interface address.

mpls ldp autoconfig

To enable Label Distribution Protocol (LDP) on interfaces for which an Open Shortest Path First (OSPF) instance has been defined, use the **mpls ldp autoconfig** command in router configuration mode.

```
mpls ldp autoconfig [ area area-id ]
```

mpls ldp discovery

To configure the interval between transmission of consecutive Label Distribution Protocol (LDP) discovery hello messages, or the hold time for a discovered LDP neighbor, or the neighbors from which requests for targeted hello messages may be honored, use the **mpls ldp discovery** command in global configuration mode.

```
mpls ldp discovery { hello { holdtime | interval } seconds |
```

```
targeted-hello { holdtime | interval } seconds | accept [ from acl
] }
```

hello	Configures the intervals and hold times for directly connected neighbors.
holdtime	Defines the period of time a discovered LDP neighbor is remembered without receipt of an LDP hello message from the neighbor. The default value for the holdtime keyword is 15 seconds for link hello messages and 90 seconds for targeted hello messages.
interval	Defines the period of time between the sending of consecutive hello messages. The default value for the interval keyword is 5 seconds for link hello messages and 10 seconds for targeted hello messages.
seconds	Hold time or interval in seconds: • The default hold time is 15 seconds for link hello messages and 90 seconds for targeted hello messages. • The default interval is 5 seconds for link hello messages and 10 seconds for targeted hello messages.
targeted-hello	Configures the intervals and hold times for neighbors that are not directly connected (for example, LDP sessions that run between the endpoints of an LSP tunnel).
accept	Configures the router to respond to requests for targeted hello messages from all neighbors or from neighbors specified by the optional acl argument.
from acl	(Optional) The IP access list that specifies the neighbor from which requests for targeted hello messages may be honored. Caution: Ensure that the access control list (ACL) is properly configured with the LDP sessions to be accepted. If no LDP entries are configured in the ACL, the ACL will allow all LDP sessions from any source.

mpls ldp explicit-null

To cause a router to advertise an Explicit Null label in situations where it would normally advertise an Implicit Null label, use the **mpls ldp explicit-null** command in global configuration mode.

```
mpls ldp explicit-null [ for prefix-acl | to peer-acl | for
prefix-acl to peer-acl ]
```

for prefix-acl	(Optional) Specifies prefixes for which Explicit Null should be advertised in place of Implicit Null.
to peer-acl	(Optional) Specifies Label Distribution Protocol (LDP) peers to which Explicit Null should be advertised in place of Implicit Null.

Implicit Null is advertised for directly connected routes unless the command mpls ldp explicit-null has been executed.

mpls ldp holdtime

To change the time for which an Label Distribution Protocol (LDP) session is maintained in the absence of LDP messages from the session peer, use the **mpls ldp holdtime** command in global configuration mode.

```
mpls ldp holdtime seconds
```

seconds	Number from 15 to 65535 that defines the time, in seconds, an LDP session is maintained in the absence of LDP messages from the session peer. The default is 180.

mpls ldp igp autoconfig

To enable Multiprotocol Label Switching (MPLS) Label Distribution Protocol (LDP) auto configuration on an interface that belongs to an Open Shortest Path First (OSPF) area, use the **mpls ldp igp autoconfig** command in interface configuration mode. To disable MPLS LDP auto configuration, use the no form of the command.

```
mpls ldp igp autoconfig
no mpls ldp igp autoconfig
```

This command works with the **mpls ldp autoconfig** command, which enables LDP on all interfaces that belong to an OSPF area. So, by default, all interfaces are enabled for LDP. To disable LDP on selected interfaces, use the **no mpls ldp igp autoconfig** command.

mpls ldp label

To enter MPLS LDP label configuration mode to specify how Multiprotocol Label Switching (MPLS) Label Distribution Protocol (LDP) handles local label allocation, use the **mpls ldp label** command in global configuration mode.

```
mpls ldp label
```

After you enter the **mpls ldp label** command, you can specify a prefix list or host routes to filter prefixes for MPLS LDP local label allocation. A maximum of one filter configuration is allowed for the global table.

allocate

To configure local label allocation filters for learned routes for Multiprotocol Label Switching (MPLS) Label Distribution Protocol (LDP), use the allocate command in MPLS LDP label configuration mode.

```
allocate global { prefix-list { list-name | list-number } |
host-routes }
```

global	Specifies the global routing table.
prefix-list	Specifies a prefix list to be used as a filter for MPLS LDP local label allocation.
list-name	Name that identifies the prefix list.
list-number	Number that identifies the prefix list.
host-routes	Specifies that host routes be used as a filter for MPLS LDP local label allocation.

mpls ldp neighbor labels accept

To configure a label switching router (LSR) to filter label distribution protocol (LDP) inbound label bindings from a particular LDP peer, use the **mpls ldp neighbor labels accept** command in global configuration mode.

```
mpls ldp neighbor [ vrf vrf-name ] nbr-address labels accept acl
```

vrf *vrf-name*	(Optional) Specifies VPN routing and forwarding instance (VRF-NAME) for accepting labels.
nbr-address	Specifies address of the LDP peer whose advertisements are to be filtered.
labels accept *acl*	Specifies the prefixes (access control list) that are acceptable (permitted).

mpls ldp neighbor password

To configure a password for computing message digest algorithm 5 (MD5) checksums for the session TCP connection with the specified neighbor, use the **mpls ldp neighbor password** command in global configuration mode.

```
mpls ldp neighbor [ vrf vrf-name ] ip-address password password
```

vrf *vrf-name*	(Optional) VPN routing and forwarding instance for the specified neighbor.
ip-address	Router ID (IP address) that identifies a neighbor.
password	Password used for computing MD5 checksums for the session TCP connection with the specified neighbor.

mpls ldp neighbor targeted

To set up a targeted session with a specified neighbor, use the **mpls ldp neighbor targeted** command in global configuration mode.

```
mpls ldp neighbor [ vrf vrf-name ] ip-addr targeted [ ldp | tdp ]
```

vrf *vrf-*	(Optional) VPN routing and forwarding (VRF) instance for

name	a specified neighbor.
ip-addr	Router ID (IP address) that identifies a neighbor.
ldp	(Optional) Specifies Label Distribution Protocol (LDP) as the label protocol for the targeted session.
tdp	(Optional) Specifies Tag Distribution Protocol (TDP) as the label protocol for the targeted session.

mpls ldp password required

To specify that Label Distribution Protocol (LDP) must use a password for an attempt to establish a session between LDP peers, use the **mpls ldp password required** command in global configuration mode.

```
mpls ldp [ vrf vrf-name ] password required [ for acl ]
```

vrf *vrf-name*	(Optional) Specifies a Virtual Private Network (VPN) routing and forwarding (VRF) instance configured on the label switch router (LSR).
for *acl*	(Optional) Access list name or number that specifies a password is mandatory only for LDP sessions with neighbors whose LDP router IDs are permitted by the list. Only standard IP access lists can be used for the acl argument.

mpls ldp router-id

To specify a preferred interface for the Label Distribution Protocol (LDP) router ID, use the mpls ldp router-id command in global configuration mode.

```
mpls ldp router-id [ vrf vrf-name ] interface [force]
```

vrf vrf-name	(Optional) Selects the interface as the LDP router ID for the named Virtual Private Network (VPN) routing

	and forwarding (VRF) table. The selected interface must be associated with the named VRF.
interface	The specified interface to be used as the LDP router ID, provided that the interface is operational.
gigabitethernet slot /subslot/port	Specifies the location of the Gigabit Ethernet interface.
force	(Optional) Alters the behavior of the mpls ldp router-id command, as described in the "Usage Guidelines" section.

If the mpls ldp router-id command is not executed, the router determines the LDP router ID as follows:

1. The router examines the IP addresses of all operational interfaces.

2. If these IP addresses include loopback interface addresses, the router selects the largest loopback address as the LDP router ID.

3. Otherwise, the router selects the largest IP address pertaining to an operational interface as the LDP router ID.

mpls mtu

To set the per-interface Multiprotocol Label Switching (MPLS) maximum transmission unit (MTU) for labeled packets, or to set the maximum MTU on the L3VPN profile, use the **mpls mtu** command in interface configuration mode or L3VPN encapsulation configuration mode respectively.

```
mpls mtu [override] bytes
```

override	(Optional) Allows you to set the MPLS MTU to a value higher than the interface MTU value on interfaces (such as Ethernet) that have a default interface MTU value of 1580 or less. The override keyword is not available for interface types that do not have a default MTU value of 1580 or less.
bytes	The MTU in bytes includes the label stack in the value.
max	Sets the MPLS MTU value to the maximum value in Generic Router Encapsulation (GRE) tunnels and L3VPN profiles.

mpls static binding ipv4

To bind a prefix to a local or remote label, use the **mpls static binding ipv4** command in global configuration mode.

```
mpls static binding ipv4 prefix mask { label | input label |
output nexthop { explicit-null | implicit-null | label } }
```

prefix mask	Specifies the prefix and mask to bind to a label. (When you do not use the input or output keyword, the specified label is an incoming label.)
	Note Without the arguments, the no form of the command removes all static bindings.
label	Binds a prefix or a mask to a local (incoming) label. (When you do not use the input or output keyword, the specified label is an incoming label.)
input *label*	Binds the specified label to the prefix and mask as a local (incoming) label.
output *nexthop* **explicit-null**	Binds the Internet Engineering Task Force (IETF) Multiprotocol Label Switching (MPLS) IPv4 explicit null label (0) as a remote (outgoing) label.
output *nexthop* **implicit-null**	Binds the IETF MPLS implicit null label (3) as a remote (outgoing) label.
output *nexthop* **label**	Binds the specified label to the prefix/mask as a remote (outgoing) label.

MPLS Troubleshooting Tools

Like other protocols, to be able to troubleshoot MPLS you need an understanding of how the protocol works. The preceding sections should help build that understanding. To help understand what you're looking at with the different show and debug commands.

Show Commands

The **show mpls ip binding** and **show mpls ldp bindings** will display the Label Information Base (LIB), just in slightly different formats.
The **show mpls forwarding-table** will display the Label Forwarding Information Base (LFIB).
The **show mpls ldp neighbor** will display the status of the LDP peer sessions.
The **show mpls ldp capabilities** will display the Label Distribution Protocol (LDP) capability information.
The **show mpls static binding** will show the static IPv4 to label bindings.
The **show ip cef** to show the contents of the FIB.
The **show ip bgp labels** command will show labels that BGP is generating or receiving for the BGP routes.

Debug Commands

The **debug mpls ldp bindings** command will display information about addresses and label bindings learned from Label Distribution Protocol (LDP) peers by means of LDP downstream unsolicited label distribution.
The **debug mpls ldp advertisements** will display information about the advertisement of labels and interface addresses to label distribution protocol (LDP) peers.
The **debug mpls events** will display information about significant Multiprotocol Label Switching (MPLS) events.
The **debug mpls packets** will display Multiprotocol Label Switching (MPLS) labeled packets switched by the host router.
So, what could they mess with in the troubleshooting section of the CCIE R&S lab relative to MPLS? They could mess with which interface(s) are configured for MPLS; which interfaces are part of which VRF; the route targets or route distinguisher within the VRF; the routing context for the VRFs; authentication for LDP; which labels are being advertised; import or export maps; static mappings of labels to IPv4 addressing; the router IDs for LDP; filters between the LSR blocking LDP...the list goes on. The following is a particularly interesting scenario...
Complaint that traffic is not passing through the MPLS cloud. When you check, you see that labels are being passed. The LDP peers seem to be fine. BGP peering is up between the PE routers and there are routes learned...but the path is not passing traffic?

Check to see how the loopbacks of the PE routers are being advertised. This is a sneaky CCIE trick that I've seen in several practice labs. The PE routers are using loopbacks to peer BGP to. OSPF is used within the MPLS cloud to provide PE to PE reachability. The PE have /24 on Loopback. The issue turns out to be an OSPF problem. OSPF by default advertises loopbacks as /32, not their configured mask. Why is this a problem? Routers generate a label for entries in the RIB/FIB, not what's being advertised. The PE has the /24 in its RIB/FIB for the loopback and therefore generates a label for that. The next hop P routers have a /32 version of the route in their RIB/FIB, therefore generates a label for a different route. The first P router doesn't get a label for the /32 route from the PE. If there's no outgoing label, the router will pop the label/labels, exposing the IP header; at that point the P router tries to route based on the IP destination. For the BGP relationship, the P router can get the packet to the PE using normal IP forwarding. The problem is that when traffic is going to a network that was learned through BGP, the PE router imposing the labels adds an outside label based on the /32 version of the route. When those packets get to the P router that has no outgoing label for the /32, it pops the label. Now it can see the underlying label, which has no meaning to that P router, so it pops that as well. It now exposes the IP header, but it doesn't have a route to the destination address so it discards. How do you fix this "MPLS" problem? Go to the PE router and add **ip ospf network point-to-point** under the loopback interface used to peer BGP. A MPLS problem that is not an MPLS problem. It is subtle, it's hard to pick up that the P router doesn't have an outgoing label for the /32 route from the PE...it's there, but it's hard to recognize the issue.

MPLS Ping and MPLS Traceroute

ICMP ping and traceroute are often used to help diagnose the root cause when a forwarding failure occurs. However, they are not well suited for identifying LSP failures because an ICMP packet can be forwarded via IP to the destination when an LSP breakage occurs.
The MPLS LSP Ping/Traceroute for LDP, and LSP Ping for VCCV feature is well suited for identifying LSP breakages for the following reasons:

- An MPLS echo request packet cannot be forwarded via IP because IP TTL is set to 1 and the IP destination address field is set to a 127/8 address.

- The FEC being checked is not stored in the IP destination address field (as is the case of ICMP).

MPLS echo request and reply packets test LSPs. There are two methods by which a downstream router can receive packets:

- The Cisco implementation of MPLS echo request and echo reply that was previously based on the Internet Engineering Task Force (IETF) Internet Draft *Detecting MPLS Data Plane Failures* (draft-ietf-mpls-lsp-ping-03.txt). This is documented in the "MPLS Embedded Management—LSP Ping/Traceroute and AToM VCCV" feature module.
- Features described in this document that are based on the IETF RFC 4379 *Detecting Multi-Protocol Label Switched (MPLS) Data Plane Failures*:
  - Echo request output interface control
  - Echo request traffic pacing
  - Echo request end-of-stack explicit-null label shimming
  - Echo request request-dsmap capability
  - Request-fec checking
  - Depth limit reporting

MPLS LSP Ping Operation

MPLS LSP ping uses MPLS echo request and reply packets to validate an LSP. You can use MPLS LSP ping to validate IPv4 LDP, AToM, and IPv4 RSVP FECs by using appropriate keywords and arguments with the **ping mpls** command.

The MPLS echo request packet is sent to a target router through the use of the appropriate label stack associated with the LSP to be validated. Use of the label stack causes the packet to be forwarded over the LSP itself.

The destination IP address of the MPLS echo request packet is different from the address used to select the label stack. The destination IP address is defined as a 127.X.Y.Z/8 address. The 127.X.Y.Z/8 address prevents the IP packet from being IP switched to its destination if the LSP is broken.

An MPLS echo reply is sent in response to an MPLS echo request. The reply is sent as an IP packet and it is forwarded using IP, MPLS, or a combination of both types of switching. The source address of the MPLS echo reply packet is an address obtained from the router generating the echo reply. The destination address is the source address of the router that originated the MPLS echo request packet. The MPLS echo reply destination port is set to the echo request source port.

Echo Reply Return Codes

Output Code	Echo Return Code	Meaning
x	0	No return code.
M	1	Malformed echo request.
m	2	Unsupported TLVs.
!	3	Success.
F	4	No FEC mapping.
D	5	DS Map mismatch.
I	6	Unknown Upstream Interface index.
U	7	Reserved.
L	8	Labeled output interface.
B	9	Unlabeled output interface.
f	10	FEC mismatch.
N	11	No label entry.
P	12	No receive interface label protocol.
p	13	Premature termination of the LSP.
X	unknown	Undefined return code.

MPLS LSP traceroute uses MPLS echo request and reply packets to validate an LSP. You can use MPLS LSP traceroute to validate IPv4 LDP and IPv4 RSVP FECs by using appropriate keywords and arguments with the **trace mpls** command.

The MPLS LSP Traceroute feature uses TTL settings to force expiration of the TTL along an LSP. MPLS LSP Traceroute incrementally increases the TTL value in its MPLS echo requests (TTL = 1, 2, 3, 4) to discover the downstream mapping of each successive hop. The success of the LSP traceroute depends on the transit router processing the MPLS echo request when it receives a labeled packet with a TTL = 1. On Cisco routers, when the TTL expires, the packet is sent to the Route Processor (RP) for processing. The transit router returns an MPLS echo reply containing information about the transit hop in response to the TTL-expired MPLS packet.

The MPLS echo reply destination port is set to the echo request source port. LSP ping drafts after Version 3 (draft-ietf-mpls-ping-03) have undergone numerous TLV format changes, but the versions of the draft do not always interoperate.

To allow later Cisco implementations to interoperate with draft Version 3 Cisco and non-Cisco implementations, a global configuration mode lets you encode and decode echo packets in formats understood by draft Version 3 implementations. Unless configured otherwise, a Cisco implementation encodes and decodes echo requests assuming the version on which the IETF implementations is based.

To prevent failures reported by the replying router due to TLV version issues, you should configure all routers in the core. Encode and decode MPLS echo packets in the same draft version. For example, if the network is running RFC 4379 (Cisco Version 4) implementations but one router is capable of only Version 3 (Cisco Revision 3), configure all routers in the network to operate in Revision 3 mode.

The Cisco implementation of MPLS echo request and echo reply is based on the IETF RFC 4379. IEFT drafts subsequent to this RFC (drafts 3, 4, 5, 6, and 7) introduced TLV format differences. These differences could not be identified because the echo packet had no way to differentiate between one TLV format and another TLV format. This introduced limited compatibility between the MPLS LSP Ping/Traceroute implementations in the Cisco IOS 12.0(27)S1 and 12.0(27)S2 releases and the MPLS ping or traceroute implementation in later Cisco IOS releases. To allow interoperability between these releases, a **revision** keyword was added for the **ping mpls** and **trace mpls** commands. The **revision** keyword enables Cisco IOS releases to support the existing draft changes and any changes from future versions of the IETF LSP Ping draft.

It's recommend that you use the mpls oam global configuration command instead of the revision option.

Cisco implementations Revision 1 and Revision 2 correspond to draft Version 3, but they contain variations of the TLV encoding. Only Cisco IOS Release 12.0(27)S1 and S2 images encode packets in Revision 1 format. No images are available on cisco.com to support Revision 2. It is recommended that you use only images supporting Version 3 and later when configuring TLV encode and decode modes. MPLS Multipath LSP traceroute requires Cisco Revision 4 or later.

Cisco Vendor Extensions

In Cisco's Version 3 (draft-ietf-mpls-ping-03.txt) implementations, Cisco defined a vendor extension TLV in the ignore-if-not-understood TLV space. It is used for the following purposes:

- Provide an ability to track TLV versions.
- Provide an experimental Reply TOS capability.

The first capability was defined before the existence of the global configuration command for setting the echo packet encode and decode behavior. TLV version information in an echo packet overrides the configured decoding behavior. Using this TLV for TLV versions is no longer required since the introduction of the global configuration capability.

The second capability controls the reply DSCP. Draft Version 8 defines a Reply TOS TLV, so the use of the reply DSCP is no longer required.

To enable compatibility between the MPLS LSP and ping or traceroute implementation by customizing the default behavior of echo packets, perform the following steps.

1. mpls oam

2. echo revision {3 | 4}

3. echo vendor-extension

	Command or Action	Purpose
Step 1	mpls oam Example: Router(config)# mpls oam	Enter MPLS OAM configuration mode for customizing the default behavior of echo packets.
Step 2	echo revision {3	4} Example: Router(config-mpls)# echo revision 4	Specifies the revision number of the echo packet's default values. • 3—draft-ietf-mpls-ping-03 (Revision 2). • 4—RFC 4379 Compliant (Default).
Step 3	echo vendor-extension Example: Router(config-mpls)# echo vendor-extension	Sends the Cisco-specific extension of TLVs with echo packets.

MPLS Ping

To check MPLS label switched path connectivity, use the **ping mpls** command in privileged EXEC mode.

```
ping mpls { ipv4 destination-address/destination-mask-
length [ destination address-start address-end increment ]
```

```
{ ttl time-to-live } | pseudowire ipv4-address vc-id [ segment
[ segment-number ] ] [ destination address-start address-
end increment ] | traffic-eng tunnel-interface tunnel-
number [ ttl time-to-live ] } [ revision { 1 | 2 | 3 | 4 } ] [
source source-address ] [ repeat count ] [ timeout seconds ] [
size packet-size | minimum maximum size-increment ] [ pad
pattern ] [ reply dscp dscp-value ] [ reply pad-tlv ] [ reply
mode { ipv4 | router-alert } ] [ interval ms ] [ exp exp-bits ] [
verbose ] [ revision tlv-revision-number ] [ force-explicit-null
] [ output interface tx-interface [ nexthop ip-address ] ] [
dsmap [ hashkey { none | ipv4 bitmap bitmap-size } ] ] [ flags fec
]
```

ipv4	Specifies the destination type as a Label Distribution Protocol (LDP) IPv4 address.
destination-address	Address prefix of the target to be tested.
/ destination-mask-length	Number of bits in the network mask of the target address. The slash is required.
destination	(Optional) Specifies a network 127 address.
address-start	(Optional) Beginning network 127 address.
address-end	(Optional) Ending network 127 address.
increment	(Optional) Number by which to increment the network 127 address.
ttl time-to-live	(Optional) Specifies a time-to-live (TTL) value. The default is 225 seconds.
pseudowire	Specifies the destination type as an Any Transport over MPLS (AToM) virtual circuit (VC).
ipv4-address	IPv4 address of the AToM VC to be tested.
vc-id	Specifies the VC identifier of the AToM VC to be tested.
segment segment-number	(Optional) Specifies a segment of a multi segment pseudowire.
traffic-eng	Specifies the destination type as an MPLS traffic engineering (TE) tunnel.
tunnel-interface	Tunnel interface to be tested.
tunnel-number	Tunnel interface number.
revision {1 | 2 | 3 | 4}	(Optional) Selects the type, length, values (TLVs) version of the implementation. Use the revision 4 as the default

	unless attempting to interoperate with devices running Cisco IOS Release 12.0(27)S1 or 12.0(27)S2. If you do not select a revision keyword, the software uses the latest version.
source source-address	(Optional) Specifies the source address or name. The default address is loopback0. This address is used as the destination address in the MPLS echo response.
repeat *count*	(Optional) Specifies the number of times to resend the same packet. The range is 1 to 2147483647. The default is 1. If you do not enter the repeat keyword, the software resends the same packet five times.
timeout *seconds*	(Optional) Specifies the timeout interval in seconds for an MPLS request packet. The range is 0 to 3600. The default is 2 seconds.
size packet-size	(Optional) Specifies the size of the packet with the label stack imposed. Packet size is the number of bytes in each ping. The range is 40 to 18024. The default is 100.
sweep	(Optional) Enables you to send a number of packets of different sizes, ranging from a start size to an end size. This parameter is similar to the Internet Control Message Protocol (ICMP) ping sweep parameter.
minimum	(Optional) Minimum or start size for an MPLS echo packet. The lower boundary of the sweep range varies depending on the LSP type. The default is 100 bytes.
maximum	(Optional) Maximum or end size for an echo packet. The default is 17,986 bytes.
size-increment	(Optional) Number by which to increment the echo packet size. The default is 100 bytes.
pad pattern	(Optional) The pad TLV is used to fill the datagram so that the MPLS echo request (User Datagram Protocol [UDP] packet with a label stack) is the specified size. The default is 0xABCD.
reply dscp *dscp-value*	(Optional) Provides the capability to request a specific class of service (CoS) in an echo reply by providing a differentiated services code point (DSCP) value. The echo reply is returned with the IP header type of service (ToS) byte set to the value specified in the reply dscp command.
reply pad-tlv	(Optional) Tests the ability of the sender of an echo

	reply to support the copy pad TLV to echo reply.
reply mode {ipv4 | router-alert}	(Optional) Specifies the reply mode for the echo request packet. ipv4 --Reply with an IPv4 UDP packet (default). router-alert --Reply with an IPv4 UDP packet with router alert.
interval *ms*	(Optional) Specifies the time, in milliseconds (ms), between successive MPLS echo requests. This parameter allows you to pace the transmission of packets so that the receiving router does not drop packets. Default is 0.
exp exp-bits	(Optional) Specifies the MPLS experimental field value in the MPLS header for an MPLS echo reply. The range is 0 to 7. Default is 0.
verbose	(Optional) Displays the MPLS echo reply sender address of the packet and displays return codes.
revision tlv-revision-number	(Optional) Cisco TLV revision number.
force-explicit-null	(Optional) Forces an explicit null label to be added to the MPLS label stack even though the label was unsolicited.
output interface *tx-interface*	(Optional) Specifies the output interface for echo requests.
nexthop ip-address	(Optional) Causes packets to go through the specified next-hop address.
dsmap	(Optional) Interrogates a transit router for downstream mapping (DSMAP) information.
hashkey {none | ipv4 bitmap *bitmap-size*}	(Optional) Allows you to control the hash key and multipath settings. Valid values are: **none** --There is no multipath (type 0). **ipv4bitmap** bitmap-size--Size of the IPv4 addresses (type 8) bitmap. If you enter the none keyword, multipath LSP traceroute acts like enhanced LSP traceroute; that is, it uses multipath LSP traceroute retry logic and consistency checking.
flags fec	(Optional) Allows Forward Equivalence Class (FEC) checking on the transit router. A downstream map TLV containing the correct received labels must be present

	in the echo request for target FEC stack checking to be performed. Target FEC stack validation is always done at the egress router. Be sure to use this keyword with the ttl keyword.

Use the **ping mpls** command to validate, test, or troubleshoot IPv4 LDP LSPs, IPv4 Resource Reservation Protocol (RSVP) TE tunnels, and AToM VCs.

With the introduction of Cisco IOS-XE Release 3.6, the interval keyword value range changed from 0 to 3,600,000 ms to 0 or 100 to 3,600,000 ms between successive MPLS echo requests.

UDP Destination Address Usage

The destination address is a valid 127/8 address. You have the option to specify a single *x.y.z-address* or a range of numbers from 0.0.0 to *x.y.z*, where *x*, *y*, and *z* are numbers from 0 to 255 and correspond to the 127.*x.y.z* destination address.

The MPLS echo request destination address in the UDP packet is not used to forward the MPLS packet to the destination router. The label stack that is used to forward the echo request routes the MPLS packet to the destination router. The 127/8 address guarantees that the packets are routed to the local host (the default loopback address of the router processing the address) if the UDP packet destination address is used for forwarding.

In addition, the destination address is used to adjust load balancing when the destination address of the IP payload is used for load balancing.

Time-to-Live Usage

The time-to-live value indicates the maximum number of hops a packet should take to reach its destination. The value in the TTL field in a packet is decremented by 1 each time the packet travels through a router.

For MPLS LSP ping, the TTL is a value after which the packet is discarded and an MPLS echo reply is sent back to the originating router.

For MPLS multipath LSP traceroute, the TTL is a maximum time-to-live value and is used to discover the number of downstream hops to the destination router. MPLS LSP traceroute incrementally increases the TTL value in its MPLS echo requests (TTL = 1, 2, 3, 4, ...) to accomplish this.

Downstream Map TLVs

The presence of a downstream map in an echo request is interpreted by the responding transit (not egress) router to include downstream map information in the echo reply. Specify the ttl and dsmap keywords to cause TTL expiry during LSP ping to interrogate a transit router for downstream information.

```
R1#ping mpls ipv4 4.4.4.0/24
Sending 5, 100-byte MPLS Echos to to 4.4.4.0/24,
    timeout is 2 seconds, send interval is 0 msec:
Codes: '!' - success, 'Q' - request not sent, '.' - timeout,
  'L' - labeled output interface, 'B' - unlabeled output interface,
  'D' - DS Map mismatch, 'F' - no FEC mapping, 'f' - FEC mismatch,
  'M' - malformed request, 'm' - unsupported tlvs, 'N' - no label
entry,
```

```
 'P' - no rx intf label prot, 'p' - premature termination of LSP,
 'R' - transit router, 'I' - unknown upstream index,
 'l' - Label switched with FEC change, 'd' - see DDMAP for return
code,
 'X' - unknown return code, 'x' - return code 0
Type escape sequence to abort.
!!!!!
Success   rate   is   100   percent   (5/5),   round-trip   min/avg/max   =
740/816/868 ms
 Total Time Elapsed 4160 ms
```

MPLS Traceroute

To discover MPLS LSP routes that packets actually take when traveling to their
destinations, use the **traceroute mpls** command in privileged EXEC mode.

```
traceroute mpls { ipv4 destination-address/destination-mask-
length  |  traffic-eng  Tunnel  tunnel-number  |  pseudowire
destination-address   vc-id  segment   segment-number   [
segment-number ] | tp } [ timeout seconds ] [ destination
address-start [ address-end | increment ] ] [ revision { 1 |
2 | 3 | 4 } ] [ source source-address ] [ exp exp-bits ] [ ttl
maximum-time-to-live ] [ reply { dscp dscp-bits | mode
reply-mode { ipv4 | no-reply | router-alert } | pad-tlv } ] [
force-explicit-null ] [ output interface tx-interface [ nexthop
ip-address ] ] [ flags fec ] [ revision tlv-revision-number ]
```

ipv4	Specifies the destination type as a Label Distribution Protocol (LDP) IPv4 address.
destination-address	Address prefix of the target to be tested.
/ destination-mask-length	Number of bits in the network mask of the target address. The slash is required.
traffic-eng Tunnel tunnel-number	Specifies the destination type as an MPLS traffic engineering (TE) tunnel.
pseudowire	Specifies the destination type as an Any Transport over MPLS (AToM) virtual circuit (VC).
tp	Verifies MPLS-TP connectivity by displaying TP tunnel identifiers throughout the path.
ipv4-address	IPv4 address of the AToM VC to be tested.
vc-id	Specifies the VC identifier of the AToM VC to be tested.

segment	Specifies a segment of a multi segment pseudowire.
segment-number	A specific segment of the multi segment pseudowire or a range of segments, indicated by two segment numbers.
timeout *seconds*	(Optional) Specifies the timeout interval in seconds. The range is from 0 to 3600. The default is 2 seconds.
destination	(Optional) Specifies a network 127 address.
address-start	(Optional) The beginning network 127 address.
address-end	(Optional) The ending network 127 address.
address-increment	(Optional) Number by which to increment the network 127 address.
revision {1 | 2 | 3| 4}	(Optional) Selects the type, length, values (TLVs) version of the implementation. Use the revision 4 default unless attempting to interoperate with devices running Cisco IOS Release 12.0(27)S1 or 12.0(27)S2. If you do not select a revision keyword, the software uses the latest version.
source source-address	(Optional) Specifies the source address or name. The default address is loopback0. This address is used as the destination address in the MPLS echo response.
exp exp-bits	(Optional) Specifies the MPLS experimental field value in the MPLS header for an MPLS echo reply. Valid values are from 0 to 7. Default is 0.
ttl maximum-time-to-live	(Optional) Specifies a maximum hop count. Default is 30.
reply dscp dscp-bits	(Optional) Provides the capability to request a specific class of service (CoS) in an echo reply by providing a differentiated services code point (DSCP) value. The echo reply is returned with the IP header ToS byte set to the value specified in the reply dscp keyword.
reply mode reply-mode	(Optional) Specifies the reply mode for the echo request packet. The reply mode is one of the following: **ipv4** --Reply with an IPv4 User Datagram Protocol (UDP) packet (default). **no-reply** --Do not send an echo request packet in response. **router-alert** --Reply with an IPv4 UDP packet with router alert.
reply pad-tlv	(Optional) Tests the ability of the sender of an echo reply to support the copy pad TLV to echo reply.

force-explicit-null	(Optional) Forces an explicit null label to be added to the MPLS label stack even though the label was unsolicited.
output interface *tx-interface*	(Optional) Specifies the output interface for echo requests.
nexthop ip-address	(Optional) Causes packets to go through the specified next-hop address.
flags fec	(Optional) Requests that target Forwarding Equivalence Class (FEC) stack validation be done at the egress router. A downstream map TLV containing the correct received labels must be present in the echo request for target FEC stack checking to be performed. Be sure to use this keyword with the ttl keyword.
revision tlv-revision-number	(Optional) Cisco TLV revision number.

Use the **traceroute mpls** command to validate, test, or troubleshoot IPv4 LDP LSPs and IPv4 Resource Reservation Protocol (RSVP) TE tunnels.

UDP Destination Address Usage

The destination address is a valid 127/8 address. You can specify a single address or a range of numbers from 0.0.0 to *x.y.z*, where *x*, *y*, and *z* are numbers from 0 to 255 and correspond to the 127.*x.y.z* destination address.

The MPLS echo request destination address in the UDP packet is not used to forward the MPLS packet to the destination router. The label stack that is used to forward the echo request routes the MPLS packet to the destination router. The 127/8 address guarantees that the packets are routed to the local host (the default loopback address of the router processing the address) if the UDP packet destination address is used for forwarding.

In addition, the destination address is used to adjust load balancing when the destination address of the IP payload is used for load balancing.

Time-to-Live Keyword Usage

The time-to-live value indicates the maximum number of hops a packet should take to reach its destination. The value in the TTL field in a packet is decremented by 1 each time the packet travels through a router.

For MPLS LSP ping, the TTL is a value after which the packet is discarded and an MPLS echo reply is sent back to the originating router.

For MPLS Multipath LSP Traceroute, the TTL is a maximum time-to-live value and is used to discover the number of downstream hops to the destination router. MPLS LSP Traceroute incrementally increases the TTL value in its MPLS echo requests (TTL = 1, 2, 3, 4, ...) to accomplish this.

```
R1#traceroute mpls ipv4 4.4.4.0/24
Tracing MPLS Label Switched Path to 4.4.4.0/24, timeout is 2 seconds
Codes: '!' - success, 'Q' - request not sent, '.' - timeout,
```

```
'L' - labeled output interface, 'B' - unlabeled output interface,
'D' - DS Map mismatch, 'F' - no FEC mapping, 'f' - FEC mismatch,
'M' - malformed request, 'm' - unsupported tlvs, 'N' - no label
entry,
'P' - no rx intf label prot, 'p' - premature termination of LSP,
'R' - transit router, 'I' - unknown upstream index,
'l' - Label switched with FEC change, 'd' - see DDMAP for return
code,
'X' - unknown return code, 'x' - return code 0
Type escape sequence to abort.
  0 10.0.12.1 MRU 1500 [Labels: 16 Exp: 0]
L 1 10.0.12.2 MRU 1500 [Labels: 16 Exp: 0] 348 ms
L 2 10.0.13.3 MRU 1504 [Labels: implicit-null Exp: 0] 360 ms
! 3 10.0.14.4 384 ms
```

CCIE Example

The following exercises are based on the topology shown in the lab setup in Appendix B.

1)

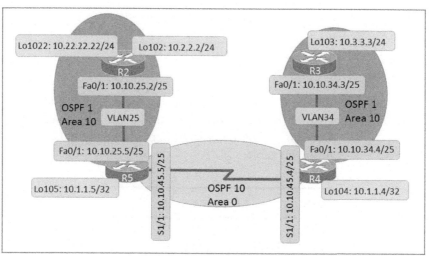

Build a baseline configuration that matches the diagram and where the following router interfaces are in area 1 for OSPF 1:

Router	Interfaces
R2	Lo102, Lo1022, Fa0/1
R3	Lo103, Fa0/1
R4	Fa0/1
R5	Fa0/1

And the following interfaces are in OSPF 10 area 0:

Router	Interfaces
R4	Lo104,S1/1
R5	Lo105, S1/1

■ Configure MPLS forwarding on the following interfaces:

Router	IPv4 Address
R4	10.10.45.4/24
R5	10.10.45.5/24

■ R4 and R5 are the label switch routers (LSRs). Use Label Distribution Protocol (LDP) for the label distribution. Configure LDP router identifiers according to the following table:

LSR	Loopback
R4	10.1.1.4/32
R5	10.1.1.5/32

■ The LDP neighbor relationship should be established between R4 and R5 respective IP addresses 10.1.1.4/32 and 10.1.1.5/32.

■ R4 should reject labels for all networks except for 10.2.2.0/24 advertised from R5.

■ Make sure that R2 can ping from Loopback 102 R3 to Loopback 103.

2)

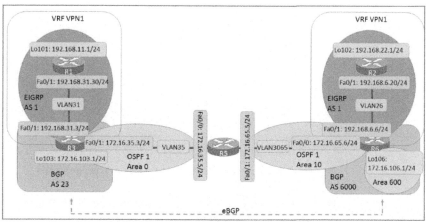

- Configure the VLANs and apply them based on the diagram.
- Configure the EIGRP AS1 neighbor relationship between R3 and R1 on VLAN 31. Advertise loopback network 192.168.11.0/24 in EIGRP AS1 on R1.
- Configure the EIGRP AS1 neighbor relationship on the 192.168.6.0/24 subnet between R6 and R2. Advertise loopback network 192.168.22.0/24 in EIGRP AS1 on R2.
- Place EIGRP AS1 in a virtual routing and forwarding (VRF) instance name VPN1 on R3 and R6, respectively.

Configure the Core IGP

- Configure R3 and R5 connection on VLAN 35 and R3 Loopback 103 in OSPF area 0.
- Configure R5 and R6 connection across VLAN3065 in OSPF area 10
- Configure R6 Loopback 106 in OSPF area 600

Configure MP-BGP

- Peer AS23 and AS6000 by establishing a peer relationship between R3 loopback interface 103 and R6 loopback interface 106.
- Provide connectivity between the VRF instance name VPN1 networks over a label switching path between R3, R5, and R6.

Make sure that R1 and R2 can ping each other from Loopback to Loopback.

3)

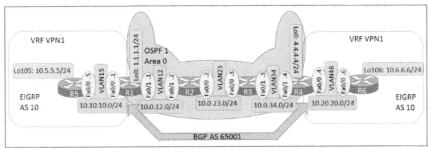

- Configure the VLANs, trunking and port assignments based on the diagram
- Configure the EIGRP AS 10 neighbor relationship between R5 and R1 on VLAN 15. Advertise loopback network 10.5.5.0/24 in EIGRP AS 10 on R5.
- Configure the EIGRP AS 10 neighbor relationship between R6 and R4 on VLAN 46. Advertise loopback network 10.6.6.0/24 in EIGRP AS 10 on R6.
- Place EIGRP AS 10 in a VRF instance name VPN1 on R1 and R4, respectively.

Core Configuration

- Configure OSPF 1 on R1, R2, R3 and R4 interconnections as area 0
- Inject Loopback 0 on R1 and R4 into OSPF area 0
- Configure an iBGP relationship between R1 and R4 using Loopback 0 as their sources

MPLS Configuration

- Enable MPLS on R1, R2, R3 and R4 interconnections
- Make sure the LDP relationships are secure using a key of C1sco
- Make sure that R3 does not perform PHP to R4

Make sure that R5 and R6 can ping others Loopback interfaces.

4)

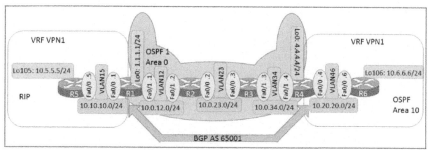

- Configure the VLANs, trunking and port assignments based on the diagram
- Configure RIPv2 between R5 and R1 on VLAN 15 and OSPF area 10 between R6 and R4 on VLAN 46.
- Place the CE IGP in a VRF instance name VPN1 on R1 and R4, respectively.

Core Configuration

- Configure OSPF 1 on R1, R2, R3 and R4 interconnections as area 0
- Inject Loopback 0 on R1 and R4 into OSPF area 0
- Configure an iBGP relationship between R1 and R4 using Loopback 0 as their sources

MPLS Configuration

- Enable MPLS on R1, R2, R3 and R4 interconnections
- Do not use multicast to discover LDP peers.
- Make sure that R2 advertises a label of 1110 for 1.1.1.0/24 and R3 advertises a label of 4440 for 4.4.4.0/24.

Make sure that R5 and R6 can ping others Loopback interfaces.

5)

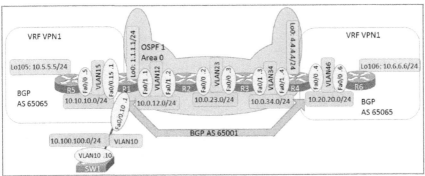

- Configure the VLANs, trunking and port assignments based on the diagram, make sure to trunk to R1 FastEthernet0/0.
- Place the interfaces feeding to R5 and R6 in a VRF instance name VPN1 on R1 and R4, respectively.
- Configure BGP between R5 and R1 on VLAN 15 and between R6 and R4 on VLAN 46.
- SW1 should have R1 as its default gateway, you are allowed to configure a static route for this on SW1.
- R1 FastEthernet0/0.10 is not in any VRF.

Core Configuration

- Configure OSPF 1 on R1, R2, R3 and R4 interconnections as area 0
- Inject Loopback 0 on R1 and R4 into OSPF area 0
- Configure an iBGP relationship between R1 and R4 using Loopback 0 as their sources

MPLS Configuration

- Enable MPLS on R1, R2, R3 and R4 interconnections
- Configure R1 such that SW1 will be able to speak to R5 and R6

Make sure that SW1 and ping R5 and R6 Loopback interfaces.

6)

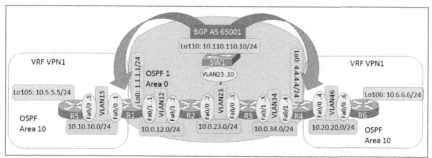

- Configure the VLANs, trunking and port assignments based on the diagram.
- Place the interfaces feeding to R5 and R6 in a VRF instance name VPN1 on R1 and R4, respectively.
- Configure OSPF Area 10 between R5 and R1 on VLAN 15 and between R6 and R4 on VLAN 46.

Core Configuration

- SW1 should have an SVI in VLAN23
- SW1 should not have any VRFs configured
- Configure OSPF 1 on R1, R2, R3,R4 and SW1 interconnections as area 0
- Inject Loopback 0 on R1, R4 and SW1 into OSPF area 0
- Configure an iBGP relationships between R1 & SW1 and R4 & SW1 using Loopback 0 to SW1 Loopback 110 as their sources, do not form a relationship between R1 and R4

MPLS Configuration

- Enable MPLS on R1, R2, R3, R4 and SW1 interconnections
- Pass the CE routes through the MPLS cloud as a Layer 3 VPN
- Make sure that R5 and R6 see the routes from each other as intra-area.

Make sure that R5 and R6 can ping others Loopback interfaces.

Appendix A – Answers

1)

You'll notice that in this exercise, there are no VRFs or BGP involved, this is a straight MPLS example where labels will (or could) be used for forwarding, rather than IPv4.

Build a baseline configuration that matches the diagram...

This part of the configuration doesn't have to be overly complicated, you just have to interpret the diagram.

```
SW2-SW#
vlan 25,34
!
interface FastEthernet1/2
 switchport access vlan 25
 duplex full
 speed 100
!
interface FastEthernet1/3
 switchport access vlan 34
 duplex full
 speed 100
!
interface FastEthernet1/4
 switchport access vlan 34
 duplex full
 speed 100
!
interface FastEthernet1/5
 switchport access vlan 25
 duplex full
 speed 100
```

...and where the following router interfaces are in area 10 for OSPF 1:

Router	Interfaces
R2	Lo102, Lo1022, Fa0/1
R3	Lo103, Fa0/1
R4	Fa0/1
R5	Fa0/1

And the following interfaces are in OSPF 10 area 0:

Router	Interfaces
R4	Lo104,S1/1
R5	Lo105, S1/1

```
R2#sh run | s router
router ospf 1
 network 10.0.0.0 0.255.255.255 area 10
R3#sh run | s router
router ospf 1
 network 10.0.0.0 0.255.255.255 area 10
R4#sh run | s router
router ospf 1
 redistribute ospf 10 subnets
 network 10.10.34.4 0.0.0.0 area 10
router ospf 10
 redistribute ospf 1 subnets
 network 10.1.1.4 0.0.0.0 area 0
 network 10.10.45.4 0.0.0.0 area 0
R5#sh run | s router
router ospf 1
 redistribute ospf 10 subnets
 network 10.10.25.5 0.0.0.0 area 10
router ospf 10
 redistribute ospf 1 subnets
 network 10.1.1.5 0.0.0.0 area 0
 network 10.10.45.5 0.0.0.0 area 0
```

- Configure MPLS forwarding on the following interfaces:

Router	IPv4 Address
R4	10.10.45.4/24
R5	10.10.45.5/24

```
R4#sh run | b 1/1
interface Serial1/1
 ip address 10.10.45.4 255.255.255.128
 mpls ip
R5#sh run | b 1/1
interface Serial1/1
 ip address 10.10.45.5 255.255.255.128
 mpls ip
```

All that's needed to start MPLS on an interface is **mpls ip**. These router should find each other automatically.

- R4 and R5 are the label switch routers (LSRs). Use Label Distribution Protocol (LDP) for the label distribution.

Configure LDP router identifiers according to the following table:

LSR	Loopback
R4	10.1.1.4/32
R5	10.1.1.5/32

```
R4#sh run | i router-id
mpls ldp router-id Loopback104
R5#sh run | i router-id
mpls ldp router-id Loopback105
```

The default section process for router ID is the same for LDP as it is for OSPF/BGP/EIGRP....look for the router ID command, if it's not there, then look for a Loopback interface and see if there is a IPv4 address on one (if there are more than one Loopback interface with IPv4 addressing, pick the one with the highest numeric value), if there is no Loopback interfaces, then select the highest numeric value of any IPv4 address on a currently up interface. In this case, the Loopback would have already been used to form the LDP peering, but this guarantees that interfaces will be used. If there was a change to the router ID, then you would have had to reset the neighbors for the new router IDs to be used.

- The LDP neighbor relationship should be established between R4 and R5 respective IP addresses 10.1.1.4/32 and 10.1.1.5/32.

- R4 should reject labels for all networks except for 10.2.2.0/24 advertised from R5.

- Make sure that R2 can ping from Loopback 102 R3 to Loopback 103.

The first bullet here is more than just using the Loopback interfaces as router IDs, it so that we use unicast to form the relationship between the peers, rather than just finding each other through the use of multicast. You use the **mpls ldp neighbor** command to identify the neighbor. The second bullet sets conditional label acceptance. This is done using a standard access list tied to the neighbor command.

```
R4#sh run | I accept|access-list
mpls ldp neighbor 10.10.45.5 labels accept 1
access-list 1 permit 10.2.2.0 0.0.0.255
R5#show mpls forwarding-table
Local      Outgoing     Prefix              Bytes Label   Outgoing    Next
```

```
Hop
Label      Label      or Tunnel Id      Switched      interface
16             No Label    10.2.2.2/32        570                      Fa0/1
10.10.25.2
17             No Label    10.22.22.22/32     0                        Fa0/1
10.10.25.2
18             Pop Label   10.1.1.4/32        0                        Se1/1
point2point
19             16          10.3.3.3/32        0                        Se1/1
point2point
20             Pop Label   10.10.34.0/25      0                        Se1/1
point2point
```

You can see from the following output that only the 10.2.2.2 has a label assigned to it from R5. The 10.22.22.22 is learned, but no label is assigned to it.

```
R4#show mpls forwarding-table
Local      Outgoing   Prefix              Bytes Label   Outgoing   Next
Hop
Label      Label      or Tunnel Id      Switched      interface
16             No Label    10.3.3.3/32        570                      Fa0/1
10.10.34.3
17             No Label    10.1.1.5/32        0                        Se1/1
point2point
18             No Label    10.22.22.22/32     0                        Se1/1
point2point
19             16          10.2.2.2/32        0                        Se1/1
point2point
20             No Label    10.10.25.0/25      0                        Se1/1
point2point
R4#
```

```
R2#ping 10.3.3.3 sou lo 102
Type escape sequence to abort.
Sending 5, 100-byte ICMP Echos to 10.3.3.3, timeout is 2 seconds:
Packet sent with a source address of 10.2.2.2
!!!!!
Success rate is 100 percent (5/5), round-trip min/avg/max =
96/109/132 ms
R2#
```

Here are the complete configurations for the routers involved:

```
R2#sh run
!
hostname R2
!
interface Loopback102
 ip address 10.2.2.2 255.255.255.0
!
interface Loopback1022
 ip address 10.22.22.22 255.255.255.0
!
interface FastEthernet0/1
 ip address 10.10.25.2 255.255.255.128
 speed auto
 duplex auto
!
router ospf 1
 network 10.0.0.0 0.255.255.255 area 10
```

```
R3#sh run
!
hostname R3
!
interface Loopback103
 ip address 10.3.3.3 255.255.255.0
!
interface FastEthernet0/1
 ip address 10.10.34.3 255.255.255.128
!
router ospf 1
 network 10.0.0.0 0.255.255.255 area 10
```
```
R4#sh run
!
hostname R4
!
mpls ldp neighbor 10.10.45.5 labels accept 1
!
interface Loopback104
 ip address 10.1.1.4 255.255.255.255
!
interface FastEthernet0/1
 ip address 10.10.34.4 255.255.255.128
!
interface Serial1/1
 ip address 10.10.45.4 255.255.255.128
 mpls ip
!
router ospf 1
 redistribute ospf 10 subnets
 network 10.10.34.4 0.0.0.0 area 10
!
router ospf 10
 redistribute ospf 1 subnets
 network 10.1.1.4 0.0.0.0 area 0
 network 10.10.45.4 0.0.0.0 area 0
!
access-list 1 permit 10.2.2.0 0.0.0.255
mpls ldp router-id Loopback104
```
```
R5#sh run
!
hostname R5
!
interface Loopback105
 ip address 10.1.1.5 255.255.255.255
!
interface FastEthernet0/1
 ip address 10.10.25.5 255.255.255.128
!
interface Serial1/1
 ip address 10.10.45.5 255.255.255.128
 mpls ip
!
router ospf 1
 redistribute ospf 10 subnets
 network 10.10.25.5 0.0.0.0 area 10
!
router ospf 10
 redistribute ospf 1 subnets
```

```
 network 10.1.1.5 0.0.0.0 area 0
 network 10.10.45.5 0.0.0.0 area 0
 !
mpls ldp router-id Loopback105
```

2)

In this exercise you had to configure a multi-domain MPLS network. This one is interesting because it involves two different BGP autonomous systems, rather than the typical single AS that we see in other examples. This would be an example of a provider MPLS network linking to another providers, passing label between them...or an Enterprise MPLS network linking to a providers MPLS network.

- Configure the VLANs and apply them based on the diagram.

Again, setting the foundation for build MPLS.

```
SW1-SW# sh run
!
hostname SW1-SW
!
vtp domain ccie
vtp mode transparent
!
vlan 26,31,35,3065
!
interface FastEthernet1/5
 switchport access vlan 35
 duplex full
 speed 100
!
interface FastEthernet1/6
 switchport access vlan 3065
 duplex full
 speed 100
!
interface FastEthernet1/11
 switchport mode trunk
 duplex full
 speed 100
!
```

```
SW2-SW#sh run
!
hostname SW2-SW
!
vtp domain ccie
vtp mode transparent
!
vlan 26,31,35,3065
!
interface FastEthernet1/1
 switchport access vlan 31
 duplex full
 speed 100
!
interface FastEthernet1/2
 switchport access vlan 26
```

```
 duplex full
 speed 100
!
interface FastEthernet1/3
 switchport mode trunk
 duplex full
 speed 100
!
interface FastEthernet1/5
 switchport access vlan 3065
 duplex full
 speed 100
!
interface FastEthernet1/6
 switchport access vlan 26
 duplex full
 speed 100
!
interface FastEthernet1/11
 switchport mode trunk
 duplex full
 speed 100
!
```

- Configure the EIGRP AS1 neighbor relationship between R3 and R1 on VLAN 31. Advertise loopback network 192.168.11.0/24 in EIGRP AS1 on R1.
- Configure the EIGRP AS1 neighbor relationship on the 192.168.6.0/24 subnet between R6 and R2. Advertise loopback network 192.168.22.0/24 in EIGRP AS1 on R2.
- Place EIGRP AS1 in a virtual routing and forwarding (VRF) instance name VPN1 on R3 and R6, respectively.

In this exercise, we're using EIGRP as the CE to PE routing protocol, so you have the chance to see different options with the different IGPs. The PE routers was now going to separate the CE routing process from the "core" IGP by using VRFs. Note that I have chosen to use the more generic version of the VRF commands in this example, even though IPv4 is the only protocol involved. I could have used the **ip vrf** command instead and that would have worked as well.

```
R1# sh run
!
hostname R1
!
interface Loopback101
 ip address 192.168.11.1 255.255.255.0
!
interface FastEthernet0/1
 ip address 192.168.31.30 255.255.255.0
 speed auto
 duplex auto
!
router eigrp 1
 network 192.168.11.1 0.0.0.0
 network 192.168.31.30 0.0.0.0
R2# sh run
!
```

```
hostname R2
!
interface Loopback102
 ip address 192.168.22.1 255.255.255.0
!
interface FastEthernet0/1
 ip address 192.168.6.20 255.255.255.0
 speed auto
 duplex auto
!
router eigrp 1
 network 192.168.22.1 0.0.0.0
 network 192.168.6.20 0.0.0.0
```
```
R3# sh run
!
hostname R3
!
vrf definition VPN1
 rd 1:1
 route-target export 1:1
 route-target import 1:1
 !
 address-family ipv4
 exit-address-family
!
interface Loopback103
 ip address 172.16.103.1 255.255.255.0
!
interface FastEthernet0/1
 no ip address
 speed auto
 duplex auto
!
interface FastEthernet0/1.31
 encapsulation dot1Q 31
 vrf forwarding VPN1
 ip address 192.168.31.3 255.255.255.0
!
interface FastEthernet0/1.35
 encapsulation dot1Q 35
 ip address 172.16.35.3 255.255.255.0
!
router eigrp 1
 !
 address-family ipv4 vrf VPN1
  network 192.168.31.3 0.0.0.0
  autonomous-system 1
 exit-address-family
 !
```
```
R6#sh run
!
hostname R6
!
vrf definition VPN1
 rd 1:1
 route-target export 1:1
 route-target import 1:1
 !
 address-family ipv4
```

```
 exit-address-family
 !
 interface Loopback106
  ip address 172.16.106.1 255.255.255.0
 !
 interface FastEthernet0/0
  ip address 172.16.65.6 255.255.255.0
  speed auto
  duplex auto
 !
 interface FastEthernet0/1
  vrf forwarding VPN1
  ip address 192.168.6.6 255.255.255.0
  speed auto
  duplex auto
 !
 router eigrp 1
  !
  address-family ipv4 vrf VPN1
   network 192.168.6.6 0.0.0.0
   auto-summary
   autonomous-system 1
  exit-address-family
 !
```

```
R3#show ip eigrp vrf VPN1 1 neighbors
EIGRP-IPv4 Neighbors for AS(1) VRF(VPN1)
H   Address                 Interface          Hold Uptime   SRTT
RTO  Q  Seq
                                               (sec)          (ms)
Cnt Num
0   192.168.31.30           Fa0/1.31             11 00:04:52 1578
5000  0  2
```

```
R6#show ip eigrp vrf VPN1 1 neighbors
EIGRP-IPv4 Neighbors for AS(1) VRF(VPN1)
H   Address                 Interface          Hold Uptime   SRTT
RTO  Q  Seq
                                               (sec)          (ms)
Cnt Num
0   192.168.6.20            Fa0/1                12 00:09:38   60
360  0  3
```

```
R3#show ip route vrf VPN1

Routing Table: VPN1
Codes: L - local, C - connected, S - static, R - RIP, M - mobile, B -
BGP
       D - EIGRP, EX - EIGRP external, O - OSPF, IA - OSPF inter area
       N1 - OSPF NSSA external type 1, N2 - OSPF NSSA external type 2
       E1 - OSPF external type 1, E2 - OSPF external type 2
       i - IS-IS, su - IS-IS summary, L1 - IS-IS level-1, L2 - IS-IS
level-2
       ia - IS-IS inter area, * - candidate default, U - per-user
static route
       o - ODR, P - periodic downloaded static route, H - NHRP, l -
LISP
       + - replicated route, % - next hop override

Gateway of last resort is not set

D     192.168.11.0/24
```

```
         [90/156160]      via      192.168.31.30,      00:06:08,
FastEthernet0/1.31
     192.168.31.0/24 is variably subnetted, 2 subnets, 2 masks
C       192.168.31.0/24 is directly connected, FastEthernet0/1.31
L       192.168.31.3/32 is directly connected, FastEthernet0/1.31
R6#show ip route vrf VPN1

Routing Table: VPN1
Codes: L - local, C - connected, S - static, R - RIP, M - mobile, B -
BGP
        D - EIGRP, EX - EIGRP external, O - OSPF, IA - OSPF inter area
        N1 - OSPF NSSA external type 1, N2 - OSPF NSSA external type 2
        E1 - OSPF external type 1, E2 - OSPF external type 2
        i - IS-IS, su - IS-IS summary, L1 - IS-IS level-1, L2 - IS-IS
level-2
        ia - IS-IS inter area, * - candidate default, U - per-user
static route
        o - ODR, P - periodic downloaded static route, H - NHRP, l -
LISP
        + - replicated route, % - next hop override

Gateway of last resort is not set

     192.168.6.0/24 is variably subnetted, 2 subnets, 2 masks
C       192.168.6.0/24 is directly connected, FastEthernet0/1
L       192.168.6.6/32 is directly connected, FastEthernet0/1
D        192.168.22.0/24 [90/156160] via 192.168.6.20,  00:10:01,
FastEthernet0/1
```

Configure the Core IGP

- Configure R3 and R5 connection on VLAN 35 and R3
  Loopback 103 in OSPF area 0.
- Configure R5 and R6 connection across VLAN3065 in OSPF
  area 10
- Configure R6 Loopback 106 in OSPF area 600

The core protocol is used for reachability between the PE routers, through any P routers. To make this more CCIE like, the OSPF topology is a bit more interesting than just a flat single area.

```
R3#sh run
!
hostname R3
!
interface Loopback103
 ip address 172.16.103.1 255.255.255.0
 ip ospf network point-to-point
!
router ospf 1
 network 172.16.35.3 0.0.0.0 area 0
 network 172.16.103.1 0.0.0.0 area 0
!
R5#sh run
!
hostname R5
!
interface FastEthernet0/0
 ip address 172.16.35.5 255.255.255.0
 speed auto
```

```
 duplex auto
 !
 interface FastEthernet0/1
  ip address 172.16.65.5 255.255.255.0
  speed auto
  duplex auto
 !
 router ospf 1
  area 10 virtual-link 172.16.106.1
  network 172.16.35.5 0.0.0.0 area 0
  network 172.16.65.5 0.0.0.0 area 10
 !
```

```
R6#sh run
 !
 hostname R6
 !
 interface Loopback106
  ip address 172.16.106.1 255.255.255.0
  ip ospf network point-to-point
 !
 router ospf 1
  area 10 virtual-link 172.16.65.5
  network 172.16.65.6 0.0.0.0 area 10
  network 172.16.106.1 0.0.0.0 area 600
 !
```

```
R3#show ip route
Codes: L - local, C - connected, S - static, R - RIP, M - mobile, B -
BGP
        D - EIGRP, EX - EIGRP external, O - OSPF, IA - OSPF inter area
        N1 - OSPF NSSA external type 1, N2 - OSPF NSSA external type 2
        E1 - OSPF external type 1, E2 - OSPF external type 2
        i - IS-IS, su - IS-IS summary, L1 - IS-IS level-1, L2 - IS-IS
level-2
        ia - IS-IS inter area, * - candidate default, U - per-user
static route
        o - ODR, P - periodic downloaded static route, H - NHRP, l -
LISP
        + - replicated route, % - next hop override

Gateway of last resort is not set

      172.16.0.0/16 is variably subnetted, 6 subnets, 2 masks
C        172.16.35.0/24 is directly connected, FastEthernet0/1.35
L        172.16.35.3/32 is directly connected, FastEthernet0/1.35
O IA        172.16.65.0/24 [110/2] via 172.16.35.5, 00:06:10,
FastEthernet0/1.35
C        172.16.103.0/24 is directly connected, Loopback103
L        172.16.103.1/32 is directly connected, Loopback103
O IA        172.16.106.0/24 [110/3] via 172.16.35.5, 00:04:10,
FastEthernet0/1.35
```

Configure MP-BGP

- Peer AS23 and AS6000 by establishing a peer relationship between R3 loopback interface 103 and R6 loopback interface 106.

- Provide connectivity between the VRF instance name VPN1 networks over a label switching path between R3, R5, and R6.

Here we are configuring the eBGP relationship between the two different autonomous systems and then establishing the label switch path. Notice that R5 is not a BGP speaker, but is configured for MPLS. It is part of the label switch path. The layer 3 VPN is being established from R3 to R6, using the eBGP relationship. Since this is an eBGP relationship where the peers are not directly attached, you have to use either **ebgp-multihop** or TTL security to get the relationship up. This is not an MPLS issue, but an eBGP issue with a default TTL of 1. For more information about BGP, see **Stupid CCIE Tricks v5.0 - section 7: BGP.** We see that we have to activate the neighbor under the address family for VPNv4 and ensure that extended communities are sent. On the PE routers you have to pass the routes from the CE into the BGP process by redistribution. Once the routes are received by the other router, they have to be passed to the CE router. Again we have to redistribute, but in this case into EIGRP. Remember that with EIGRP, if you are redistributing from something other than connected, static or another EIGRP process, you have to give the process a seed metric. In this case I used an unattractive metric of 1 1 1 1 1, but if you notice on R1, then metric isn't that bad. BGP has had extensions added to include information about the original IGP from the other PE router and Cisco has added more to include information about EIGRP, which includes the composite metrics that were used in the original routes. This is only true when this is a layer 3 VPN over MPLS. When you redistribute the BGP learned routes into EIGRP, if the original protocol was also EIGRP, then the composite metrics that BGP was carrying will be used over the configured seed metric and the routes will look like native EIGRP routes. You have to configure the seed metric to allow EIGRP to even attempt to redistribute the routes. If the original protocol was not EIGRP, the routes would should up as external and the seed metric would be used.

```
R3#sh run
!
hostname R3
!
interface FastEthernet0/1.35
 encapsulation dot1Q 35
 ip address 172.16.35.3 255.255.255.0
 mpls ip
!
router eigrp 1
 !
 address-family ipv4 vrf VPN1
  redistribute bgp 23 metric 1 1 1 1 1
  network 192.168.31.3 0.0.0.0
  autonomous-system 1
 exit-address-family
!
router bgp 23
 bgp log-neighbor-changes
 neighbor 172.16.106.1 remote-as 6000
```

```
 neighbor 172.16.106.1 ebgp-multihop 3
 neighbor 172.16.106.1 update-source Loopback103
 !
 address-family vpnv4
  neighbor 172.16.106.1 activate
  neighbor 172.16.106.1 send-community extended
 exit-address-family
 !
 address-family ipv4 vrf VPN1
  redistribute eigrp 1
 exit-address-family
!
```

```
R5#sh run
!
hostname R5
!
interface FastEthernet0/0
 ip address 172.16.35.5 255.255.255.0
 speed auto
 duplex auto
 mpls ip
!
interface FastEthernet0/1
 ip address 172.16.65.5 255.255.255.0
 speed auto
 duplex auto
 mpls ip
!
```

```
R6#sh run
!
hostname R6
!
interface FastEthernet0/0
 ip address 172.16.65.6 255.255.255.0
 speed auto
 duplex auto
 mpls ip
!
router eigrp 1
 !
 address-family ipv4 vrf VPN1
  redistribute bgp 6000 metric 1 1 1 1 1
  network 192.168.6.6 0.0.0.0
  auto-summary
  autonomous-system 1
 exit-address-family
!
router bgp 6000
 bgp log-neighbor-changes
 neighbor 172.16.103.1 remote-as 23
 neighbor 172.16.103.1 ebgp-multihop 3
 neighbor 172.16.103.1 update-source Loopback106
 !
 address-family vpnv4
  neighbor 172.16.103.1 activate
  neighbor 172.16.103.1 send-community extended
 exit-address-family
 !
 address-family ipv4 vrf VPN1
```

```
  redistribute eigrp 1
  exit-address-family
 !
```

```
R1#show ip route
Codes: L - local, C - connected, S - static, R - RIP, M - mobile, B -
BGP
       D - EIGRP, EX - EIGRP external, O - OSPF, IA - OSPF inter area
       N1 - OSPF NSSA external type 1, N2 - OSPF NSSA external type 2
       E1 - OSPF external type 1, E2 - OSPF external type 2
       i - IS-IS, su - IS-IS summary, L1 - IS-IS level-1, L2 - IS-IS
level-2
       ia - IS-IS inter area, * - candidate default, U - per-user
static route
       o - ODR, P - periodic downloaded static route, H - NHRP, l -
LISP
       + - replicated route, % - next hop override

Gateway of last resort is not set

      192.168.11.0/24 is variably subnetted, 2 subnets, 2 masks
C        192.168.11.0/24 is directly connected, Loopback101
L        192.168.11.1/32 is directly connected, Loopback101
D          192.168.22.0/24 [90/158720] via 192.168.31.3,  00:07:03,
FastEthernet0/1
      192.168.31.0/24 is variably subnetted, 2 subnets, 2 masks
C        192.168.31.0/24 is directly connected, FastEthernet0/1
L        192.168.31.30/32 is directly connected, FastEthernet0/1
```

```
R3#show ip bgp vpnv4 all
BGP table version is 4, local router ID is 172.16.103.1
Status codes: s suppressed, d damped, h history, * valid, > best, i -
internal,
              r RIB-failure, S Stale, m multipath, b backup-path, f
RT-Filter,
              x best-external, a additional-path, c RIB-compressed,
Origin codes: i - IGP, e - EGP, ? - incomplete
RPKI validation codes: V valid, I invalid, N Not found

     Network          Next Hop          Metric LocPrf Weight Path
Route Distinguisher: 1:1 (default for vrf VPN1)
 *>  192.168.11.0    192.168.31.30       156160         32768 ?
 *>  192.168.22.0    172.16.106.1        156160             0 6000 ?
```

```
R3#show mpls forwarding-table
Local     Outgoing   Prefix             Bytes Label  Outgoing    Next
Hop
Label     Label      or Tunnel Id       Switched     interface
16         Pop Label  172.16.65.0/24     0                       Fa0/1.35
172.16.35.5
17         17         172.16.106.0/24    0                       Fa0/1.35
172.16.35.5
18         No Label   192.168.11.0/24[V]    \
                                         590                     Fa0/1.31
192.168.31.30
```

```
R3#show ip bgp vpnv4 vrf VPN1 labels
   Network          Next Hop      In label/Out label
Route Distinguisher: 1:1 (VPN1)
   192.168.11.0    192.168.31.30   18/nolabel
   192.168.22.0    172.16.106.1    nolabel/18
```

```
R3#sh mpls forwarding-table vrf VPN1 192.168.22.0 detail
Local     Outgoing   Prefix             Bytes Label  Outgoing    Next
```

```
Hop
Label      Label        or Tunnel Id      Switched       interface
None       18           192.168.22.0/24[V]    \
                                          0                      Fa0/1.35
172.16.35.5
           MAC/Encaps=18/26, MRU=1496, Label Stack{17 18}
           CA0026C40008CA0924600006810000238847 0001100000012000
           VPN route: VPN1
           No output feature configured
```

Make sure that R1 and R2 can ping each other from Loopback to Loopback.

```
R1#p 192.168.22.1 sou lo 101
Type escape sequence to abort.
Sending 5, 100-byte ICMP Echos to 192.168.22.1, timeout is 2 seconds:
Packet sent with a source address of 192.168.11.1
!!!!!
Success   rate   is   100   percent   (5/5),   round-trip   min/avg/max   =
124/138/152 ms
```

Here are the configurations of the routers involved:

```
R1#show run
!
hostname R1
!
interface Loopback101
 ip address 192.168.11.1 255.255.255.0
!
interface FastEthernet0/1
 ip address 192.168.31.30 255.255.255.0
 speed auto
 duplex auto
!
!
router eigrp 1
 network 192.168.11.1 0.0.0.0
 network 192.168.31.30 0.0.0.0
!
```

```
R2#sh run
!
hostname R2
!
interface Loopback102
 ip address 192.168.22.1 255.255.255.0
!
interface FastEthernet0/1
 ip address 192.168.6.20 255.255.255.0
 speed auto
 duplex auto
!
router eigrp 1
 network 192.168.6.20 0.0.0.0
 network 192.168.22.1 0.0.0.0
!
```

```
R3#show run
!
hostname R3
!
vrf definition VPN1
 rd 1:1
 route-target export 1:1
```

```
 route-target import 1:1
 !
 address-family ipv4
 exit-address-family
!
interface Loopback103
 ip address 172.16.103.1 255.255.255.0
 ip ospf network point-to-point
!
interface FastEthernet0/1
 no ip address
 speed auto
 duplex auto
!
interface FastEthernet0/1.31
 encapsulation dot1Q 31
 vrf forwarding VPN1
 ip address 192.168.31.3 255.255.255.0
!
interface FastEthernet0/1.35
 encapsulation dot1Q 35
 ip address 172.16.35.3 255.255.255.0
 mpls ip
!
router eigrp 1
 !
 address-family ipv4 vrf VPN1
  redistribute bgp 23 metric 1 1 1 1 1
  network 192.168.31.3 0.0.0.0
  autonomous-system 1
 exit-address-family
!
router ospf 1
 network 172.16.35.3 0.0.0.0 area 0
 network 172.16.103.1 0.0.0.0 area 0
!
router bgp 23
 bgp log-neighbor-changes
 neighbor 172.16.106.1 remote-as 6000
 neighbor 172.16.106.1 ebgp-multihop 3
 neighbor 172.16.106.1 update-source Loopback103
 !
 address-family vpnv4
  neighbor 172.16.106.1 activate
  neighbor 172.16.106.1 send-community extended
 exit-address-family
 !
 address-family ipv4 vrf VPN1
  redistribute eigrp 1
 exit-address-family
!
```

```
R5#sh run
!
hostname R5
!
interface FastEthernet0/0
 ip address 172.16.35.5 255.255.255.0
 speed auto
 duplex auto
```

```
 mpls ip
 !
 interface FastEthernet0/1
  ip address 172.16.65.5 255.255.255.0
  speed auto
  duplex auto
  mpls ip
 !
 router ospf 1
  area 10 virtual-link 172.16.106.1
  network 172.16.35.5 0.0.0.0 area 0
  network 172.16.65.5 0.0.0.0 area 10
 !
```
```
R6#sh run
!
hostname R6
!
vrf definition VPN1
 rd 1:1
 route-target export 1:1
 route-target import 1:1
 !
 address-family ipv4
 exit-address-family
!
interface Loopback106
 ip address 172.16.106.1 255.255.255.0
 ip ospf network point-to-point
!
interface FastEthernet0/0
 ip address 172.16.65.6 255.255.255.0
 speed auto
 duplex auto
 mpls ip
!
interface FastEthernet0/1
 vrf forwarding VPN1
 ip address 192.168.6.6 255.255.255.0
 speed auto
 duplex auto
!
router eigrp 1
 !
 address-family ipv4 vrf VPN1
  redistribute bgp 6000 metric 1 1 1 1 1
  network 192.168.6.6 0.0.0.0
  auto-summary
  autonomous-system 1
 exit-address-family
!
router ospf 1
 area 10 virtual-link 172.16.65.5
 network 172.16.65.6 0.0.0.0 area 10
 network 172.16.106.1 0.0.0.0 area 600
!
router bgp 6000
 bgp log-neighbor-changes
 neighbor 172.16.103.1 remote-as 23
 neighbor 172.16.103.1 ebgp-multihop 3
```

```
neighbor 172.16.103.1 update-source Loopback106
!
address-family vpnv4
 neighbor 172.16.103.1 activate
 neighbor 172.16.103.1 send-community extended
exit-address-family
!
address-family ipv4 vrf VPN1
 redistribute eigrp 1
exit-address-family
!
```

3)

This is a more traditional CCIE R&S type MPLS configuration, whereas we have a single IGP for the core and we're running iBGP between the PE routers. The twists, if you can call it that are the authentication and disabling PHP...which as we know the text preceding the exercises, you really can't do.

- Configure the VLANs, trunking and port assignments based on the diagram

Another straight forward foundation to build the topology from.

```
SW1-SW# sh run
!
hostname SW1-SW
!
vtp domain ccie
vtp mode transparent
vlan 15,23,46
!
interface FastEthernet1/1
 switchport access vlan 15
 duplex full
 speed 100
!
interface FastEthernet1/2
 switchport access vlan 23
 duplex full
 speed 100
!
interface FastEthernet1/3
 switchport access vlan 23
 duplex full
 speed 100
!
interface FastEthernet1/4
 switchport access vlan 46
 duplex full
 speed 100
!
interface FastEthernet1/5
 switchport access vlan 15
 duplex full
 speed 100
!
interface FastEthernet1/6
 switchport access vlan 46
 duplex full
 speed 100
!
```
```
SW2-SW# sh run
!
hostname SW2-SW
!
```

```
vtp domain ccie
vtp mode transparent
vlan 12,34
!
interface FastEthernet1/1
 switchport access vlan 12
 duplex full
 speed 100
!
interface FastEthernet1/2
 switchport access vlan 12
 duplex full
 speed 100
!
interface FastEthernet1/3
 switchport access vlan 34
 duplex full
 speed 100
!
interface FastEthernet1/4
 switchport access vlan 34
 duplex full
 speed 100
```

- Configure the EIGRP AS 10 neighbor relationship between R5 and R1 on VLAN 15. Advertise loopback network 10.5.5.0/24 in EIGRP AS 10 on R5.
- Configure the EIGRP AS 10 neighbor relationship between R6 and R4 on VLAN 46. Advertise loopback network 10.6.6.0/24 in EIGRP AS 10 on R6.
- Place EIGRP AS 10 in a VRF instance name VPN1 on R1 and R4, respectively.

EIGRP for the CE routers and VRFs on the PE routers to support a layer 3 VPN.

```
R1#sh run
!
hostname R1
!
vrf definition VPN1
 rd 1:1
 route-target export 1:1
 route-target import 1:1
 !
 address-family ipv4
 exit-address-family
!
interface Loopback0
 ip address 1.1.1.1 255.255.255.0
!
interface FastEthernet0/0
 vrf forwarding VPN1
 ip address 10.10.10.1 255.255.255.0
 speed auto
 duplex auto
!
interface FastEthernet0/1
 ip address 10.0.12.1 255.255.255.0
 speed auto
```

```
  duplex auto
 !
router eigrp 1
 !
 address-family ipv4 vrf VPN1
  network 10.10.10.1 0.0.0.0
  autonomous-system 10
 exit-address-family
 !
```
```
R4#sh run
!
hostname R4
!
vrf definition VPN1
 rd 1:1
 route-target export 1:1
 route-target import 1:1
 !
 address-family ipv4
 exit-address-family
!
interface Loopback0
 ip address 4.4.4.4 255.255.255.0
!
interface FastEthernet0/0
 vrf forwarding VPN1
 ip address 10.20.20.4 255.255.255.0
 speed auto
 duplex auto
!
interface FastEthernet0/1
 ip address 10.0.34.4 255.255.255.0
 speed auto
 duplex auto
!
router eigrp 1
 !
 address-family ipv4 vrf VPN1
  network 10.20.20.4 0.0.0.0
  autonomous-system 10
 exit-address-family
 !
```
```
R5#show run
!
hostname R5
!
interface Loopback105
 ip address 10.5.5.5 255.255.255.0
!
interface FastEthernet0/0
 ip address 10.10.10.5 255.255.255.0
 speed auto
 duplex auto
!
router eigrp 10
 network 10.0.0.0
 !
```
```
R6#show run
```

```
!
hostname R6
!
interface Loopback106
 ip address 10.6.6.6 255.255.255.0
!
interface FastEthernet0/0
 ip address 10.20.20.6 255.255.255.0
 speed auto
 duplex auto
!
router eigrp 10
 network 10.0.0.0
!
```

Core Configuration

- Configure OSPF 1 on R1, R2, R3 and R4 interconnections as area 0
- Inject Loopback 0 on R1 and R4 into OSPF area 0
- Configure an iBGP relationship between R1 and R4 using Loopback 0 as their sources

Single area OSPF and a iBGP peering between the PE routers.

```
R1#show run
!
hostname R1
!
interface Loopback0
 ip address 1.1.1.1 255.255.255.0
 ip ospf network point-to-point
!
router ospf 1
 network 1.1.1.1 0.0.0.0 area 0
 network 10.0.0.0 0.255.255.255 area 0
!
router bgp 65001
 bgp log-neighbor-changes
 neighbor 4.4.4.4 remote-as 65001
 neighbor 4.4.4.4 update-source Loopback0
!
```

```
R2#show run
!
hostname R2
!
interface FastEthernet0/0
 ip address 10.0.23.2 255.255.255.0
 speed auto
 duplex auto
!
interface FastEthernet0/1
 ip address 10.0.12.2 255.255.255.0
 speed auto
 duplex auto
!
router ospf 1
 network 10.0.0.0 0.255.255.255 area 0
!
```

```
R3#show run
```

```
!
hostname R3
!
interface FastEthernet0/0
 ip address 10.0.23.3 255.255.255.0
 speed auto
 duplex auto
!
interface FastEthernet0/1
 ip address 10.0.34.3 255.255.255.0
 speed auto
 duplex auto
!
router ospf 1
 network 10.0.0.0 0.255.255.255 area 0
!
```

```
R4#show run
!
hostname R4
!
interface Loopback0
 ip address 4.4.4.4 255.255.255.0
!
router ospf 1
 network 4.4.4.4 0.0.0.0 area 0
 network 10.0.0.0 0.255.255.255 area 0
!
router bgp 65001
 bgp log-neighbor-changes
 neighbor 1.1.1.1 remote-as 65001
 neighbor 1.1.1.1 update-source Loopback0
!
```

MPLS Configuration

- Enable MPLS on R1, R2, R3 and R4 interconnections
- Make sure the LDP relationships are secure using a key of C1sco
- Make sure that R3 does not perform PHP to R4

Starts off as a straightforward MPLS config then we get the authentication and the PHP requirement. Note that the password is NOT Cisco, the "i" is a "1" (one). This isn't graded, but if it was and you missed it, no points-for-you! Remember that you really can't turn off PHP, but you can make the PE router not send the implicit null label, but send an explicit null.

```
R1#show run
!
hostname R1
!
mpls ldp password required
mpls ldp neighbor 10.0.23.2 password C1sco
!
interface FastEthernet0/1
 ip address 10.0.12.1 255.255.255.0
 speed auto
 duplex auto
 mpls ip
!
```

```
router eigrp 1
 !
 address-family ipv4 vrf VPN1
  redistribute bgp 65001 metric 1 1 1 1 1
  network 10.10.10.1 0.0.0.0
  autonomous-system 10
 exit-address-family
 !
router bgp 65001
 bgp log-neighbor-changes
 neighbor 4.4.4.4 remote-as 65001
 neighbor 4.4.4.4 update-source Loopback0
 !
 address-family vpnv4
  neighbor 4.4.4.4 activate
  neighbor 4.4.4.4 send-community extended
 exit-address-family
 !
 address-family ipv4 vrf VPN1
  redistribute eigrp 10
 exit-address-family
 !
```

```
R2#show run
!
hostname R2
!
mpls ldp password required
mpls ldp neighbor 10.0.34.3 password C1sco
mpls ldp neighbor 1.1.1.1 password C1sco
!
interface FastEthernet0/0
 ip address 10.0.23.2 255.255.255.0
 speed auto
 duplex auto
 mpls ip
!
interface FastEthernet0/1
 ip address 10.0.12.2 255.255.255.0
 speed auto
 duplex auto
 mpls ip
!
```

```
R3#show run
!
hostname R3
!
mpls ldp password required
mpls ldp neighbor 4.4.4.4 password C1sco
mpls ldp neighbor 10.0.23.2 password C1sco
!
interface FastEthernet0/0
 ip address 10.0.23.3 255.255.255.0
 speed auto
 duplex auto
 mpls ip
!
interface FastEthernet0/1
 ip address 10.0.34.3 255.255.255.0
```

```
 duplex auto
 mpls ip
 !
```
```
R4#show run
 !
hostname R4
 !
mpls ldp password required
mpls ldp neighbor 10.0.34.3 password C1sco
mpls ldp explicit-null
 !
interface FastEthernet0/1
 ip address 10.0.34.4 255.255.255.0
 speed auto
 duplex auto
 mpls ip
 !
router eigrp 1
 !
 address-family ipv4 vrf VPN1
  redistribute bgp 65001 metric 1 1 1 1 1
  network 10.20.20.4 0.0.0.0
  autonomous-system 10
 exit-address-family
 !
router bgp 65001
 bgp log-neighbor-changes
 neighbor 1.1.1.1 remote-as 65001
 neighbor 1.1.1.1 update-source Loopback0
 !
 address-family vpnv4
  neighbor 1.1.1.1 activate
  neighbor 1.1.1.1 send-community extended
 exit-address-family
 !
 address-family ipv4 vrf VPN1
  redistribute eigrp 10
 exit-address-family
 !
```

We can see from the output of the **show mpls forwarding-table** on R3
that it has received the explicit null from R4, so R4 will now have to POP
that label to expose the underlying VPN label.

```
R3#sh mpls forwarding-table
Local      Outgoing    Prefix           Bytes Label   Outgoing    Next
Hop
Label      Label      or Tunnel Id    Switched      interface
16          16          1.1.1.0/24              2725            Fa0/0
10.0.23.2
18          Pop Label  10.0.12.0/24     0                      Fa0/0
10.0.23.2
19          explicit-n 4.4.4.0/24              2759            Fa0/1
10.0.34.4
```
```
R3#show mpls ldp neighbor detail
    Peer LDP Ident: 10.0.23.2:0; Local LDP Ident 10.0.34.3:0
       TCP connection: 10.0.23.646 - 10.0.34.3.52740; MD5 on
```

```
           State: Oper; Msgs sent/rcvd: 36/36; Downstream; Last TIB rev
sent 16
        Up time: 00:22:12; UID: 4; Peer Id 2
        LDP discovery sources:
          FastEthernet0/0; Src IP addr: 10.0.23.2
            holdtime: 15000 ms, hello interval: 5000 ms
        Addresses bound to peer LDP Ident:
          10.0.23.2        10.0.12.2
        Peer holdtime: 180000 ms; KA interval: 60000 ms; Peer state:
estab
        Capabilities Sent:
          [ICCP (type 0x0405) MajVer 1 MinVer 0]
          [Dynamic Announcement (0x0506)]
          [mLDP Point-to-Multipoint (0x0508)]
          [mLDP Multipoint-to-Multipoint (0x0509)]
          [Typed Wildcard (0x050B)]
        Capabilities Received:
          [ICCP (type 0x0405) MajVer 1 MinVer 0]
          [Dynamic Announcement (0x0506)]
          [mLDP Point-to-Multipoint (0x0508)]
          [mLDP Multipoint-to-Multipoint (0x0509)]
          [Typed Wildcard (0x050B)]
    Peer LDP Ident: 4.4.4.4:0; Local LDP Ident 10.0.34.3:0
        TCP connection: 4.4.4.4.646 - 10.0.34.3.36094; MD5 on
        Password: required, neighbor, in use
        State: Oper; Msgs sent/rcvd: 34/38; Downstream; Last TIB rev
sent 16
        Up time: 00:17:43; UID: 6; Peer Id 0
        LDP discovery sources:
          FastEthernet0/1; Src IP addr: 10.0.34.4
            holdtime: 15000 ms, hello interval: 5000 ms
        Addresses bound to peer LDP Ident:
          10.0.34.4        4.4.4.4
        Peer holdtime: 180000 ms; KA interval: 60000 ms; Peer state:
estab
        Capabilities Sent:
          [ICCP (type 0x0405) MajVer 1 MinVer 0]
          [Dynamic Announcement (0x0506)]
          [mLDP Point-to-Multipoint (0x0508)]
          [mLDP Multipoint-to-Multipoint (0x0509)]
          [Typed Wildcard (0x050B)]
        Capabilities Received:
          [ICCP (type 0x0405) MajVer 1 MinVer 0]
          [Dynamic Announcement (0x0506)]
          [mLDP Point-to-Multipoint (0x0508)]
          [mLDP Multipoint-to-Multipoint (0x0509)]
          [Typed Wildcard (0x050B)]
```

Make sure that R5 and R6 can ping others Loopback interfaces.

```
R5#sh ip route
Codes: L - local, C - connected, S - static, R - RIP, M - mobile, B -
BGP
        D - EIGRP, EX - EIGRP external, O - OSPF, IA - OSPF inter area
        N1 - OSPF NSSA external type 1, N2 - OSPF NSSA external type 2
        E1 - OSPF external type 1, E2 - OSPF external type 2
        i - IS-IS, su - IS-IS summary, L1 - IS-IS level-1, L2 - IS-IS
level-2
        ia - IS-IS inter area, * - candidate default, U - per-user
static route
```

```
         o - ODR, P - periodic downloaded static route, H - NHRP, l -
LISP
         + - replicated route, % - next hop override

Gateway of last resort is not set

      10.0.0.0/8 is variably subnetted, 5 subnets, 2 masks
C        10.5.5.0/24 is directly connected, Loopback105
L        10.5.5.5/32 is directly connected, Loopback105
D              10.6.6.0/24 [90/158720] via 10.10.10.1, 00:25:24,
FastEthernet0/0
C        10.10.10.0/24 is directly connected, FastEthernet0/0
L        10.10.10.5/32 is directly connected, FastEthernet0/0
R5#ping 10.6.6.6 sou lo 105
Type escape sequence to abort.
Sending 5, 100-byte ICMP Echos to 10.6.6.6, timeout is 2 seconds:
Packet sent with a source address of 10.5.5.5
!!!!!
Success  rate  is  100  percent  (5/5),  round-trip  min/avg/max  =
120/170/192 ms
```

Here are the configs for all the routers involved:

```
R1#sh run
!
hostname R1
!
vrf definition VPN1
 rd 1:1
 route-target export 1:1
 route-target import 1:1
 !
 address-family ipv4
 exit-address-family
!
mpls ldp password required
mpls ldp neighbor 10.0.23.2 password C1sco
!
interface Loopback0
 ip address 1.1.1.1 255.255.255.0
 ip ospf network point-to-point
!
interface FastEthernet0/0
 vrf forwarding VPN1
 ip address 10.10.10.1 255.255.255.0
 speed auto
 duplex auto
!
interface FastEthernet0/1
 ip address 10.0.12.1 255.255.255.0
 speed auto
 duplex auto
 mpls ip
!
router eigrp 1
 !
 address-family ipv4 vrf VPN1
  redistribute bgp 65001 metric 1 1 1 1 1
  network 10.10.10.1 0.0.0.0
```

```
  autonomous-system 10
 exit-address-family
 !
 router ospf 1
  network 1.1.1.1 0.0.0.0 area 0
  network 10.0.0.0 0.255.255.255 area 0
 !
 router bgp 65001
  bgp log-neighbor-changes
  neighbor 4.4.4.4 remote-as 65001
  neighbor 4.4.4.4 update-source Loopback0
  !
  address-family vpnv4
   neighbor 4.4.4.4 activate
   neighbor 4.4.4.4 send-community extended
  exit-address-family
  !
  address-family ipv4 vrf VPN1
   redistribute eigrp 10
  exit-address-family
 !
```

```
R2#show run
!
hostname R2
!
mpls ldp password required
mpls ldp neighbor 10.0.34.3 password C1sco
mpls ldp neighbor 1.1.1.1 password C1sco
!
interface FastEthernet0/0
 ip address 10.0.23.2 255.255.255.0
 speed auto
 duplex auto
 mpls ip
!
interface FastEthernet0/1
 ip address 10.0.12.2 255.255.255.0
 speed auto
 duplex auto
 mpls ip
!
router ospf 1
 network 10.0.0.0 0.255.255.255 area 0
!
```

```
R3#show run
!
hostname R3
!
mpls ldp password required
mpls ldp neighbor 10.0.23.2 password C1sco
mpls ldp neighbor 4.4.4.4 password C1sco
!
interface FastEthernet0/0
 ip address 10.0.23.3 255.255.255.0
 speed auto
 duplex auto
 mpls ip
!
```

```
 ip address 10.0.34.3 255.255.255.0
 speed auto
 duplex auto
 mpls ip
!
router ospf 1
 network 10.0.0.0 0.255.255.255 area 0
!
```

```
R4#show run
!
hostname R4
!
vrf definition VPN1
 rd 1:1
 route-target export 1:1
 route-target import 1:1
 !
 address-family ipv4
 exit-address-family
!
mpls ldp password required
mpls ldp neighbor 10.0.34.3 password C1sco
mpls ldp explicit-null
!
interface Loopback0
 ip address 4.4.4.4 255.255.255.0
 ip ospf network point-to-point
!
interface Loopback0
 ip address 4.4.4.4 255.255.255.0
 ip ospf network point-to-point
!
interface FastEthernet0/0
 vrf forwarding VPN1
 ip address 10.20.20.4 255.255.255.0
 speed auto
 duplex auto
!
interface FastEthernet0/1
 ip address 10.0.34.4 255.255.255.0
 speed auto
 duplex auto
 mpls ip
!
router eigrp 1
 !
 address-family ipv4 vrf VPN1
  redistribute bgp 65001 metric 1 1 1 1 1
  network 10.20.20.4 0.0.0.0
  autonomous-system 10
 exit-address-family
!
router ospf 1
 network 4.4.4.4 0.0.0.0 area 0
 network 10.0.0.0 0.255.255.255 area 0
!
router bgp 65001
 bgp log-neighbor-changes
 neighbor 1.1.1.1 remote-as 65001
```

```
 neighbor 1.1.1.1 update-source Loopback0
 !
 address-family vpnv4
  neighbor 1.1.1.1 activate
  neighbor 1.1.1.1 send-community extended
 exit-address-family
 !
 address-family ipv4 vrf VPN1
  redistribute eigrp 10
 exit-address-family
!
```
```
R5# sh run
!
hostname R5
!
interface Loopback105
 ip address 10.5.5.5 255.255.255.0
!
interface FastEthernet0/0
 ip address 10.10.10.5 255.255.255.0
 speed auto
 duplex auto
!
router eigrp 10
 network 10.0.0.0
!
```
```
R6# show run
!
hostname R6
!
interface Loopback106
 ip address 10.6.6.6 255.255.255.0
!
interface FastEthernet0/0
 ip address 10.20.20.6 255.255.255.0
 speed auto
 duplex auto
!
router eigrp 10
 network 10.0.0.0
!
```

4)

This is based on the same topology as exercise 3, but the IGPs are different from one side to the other. On the R1 to R5 side it's RIP and on the R4 to R6 side it's OSPF. Otherwise the base configuration is the same.

■ Configure the VLANs, trunking and port assignments based on the diagram

```
SW1-SW# sh run
!
hostname SW1-SW
!
vtp domain ccie
vtp mode transparent
vlan 15,23,46
!
interface FastEthernet1/1
 switchport access vlan 15
 duplex full
 speed 100
!
interface FastEthernet1/2
 switchport access vlan 23
 duplex full
 speed 100
!
interface FastEthernet1/3
 switchport access vlan 23
 duplex full
 speed 100
!
interface FastEthernet1/4
 switchport access vlan 46
 duplex full
 speed 100
!
interface FastEthernet1/5
 switchport access vlan 15
 duplex full
 speed 100
!
interface FastEthernet1/6
 switchport access vlan 46
 duplex full
 speed 100
!
```

```
SW2-SW# sh run
!
hostname SW2-SW
!
vtp domain ccie
vtp mode transparent
```

```
!
interface FastEthernet1/1
 switchport access vlan 12
 duplex full
 speed 100
!
interface FastEthernet1/2
 switchport access vlan 12
 duplex full
 speed 100
!
interface FastEthernet1/3
 switchport access vlan 34
 duplex full
 speed 100
!
interface FastEthernet1/4
 switchport access vlan 34
 duplex full
 speed 100
```

- Configure RIPv2 between R5 and R1 on VLAN 15 and OSPF area 10 between R6 and R4 on VLAN 46.
- Place the CE IGP in a VRF instance name VPN1 on R1 and R4, respectively.

```
R1#sh run
!
hostname R1
!
vrf definition VPN1
 rd 1:1
 route-target export 1:1
 route-target import 1:1
 !
 address-family ipv4
 exit-address-family
!
interface Loopback0
 ip address 1.1.1.1 255.255.255.0
!
interface FastEthernet0/0
 vrf forwarding VPN1
 ip address 10.10.10.1 255.255.255.0
 speed auto
 duplex auto
!
interface FastEthernet0/1
 ip address 10.0.12.1 255.255.255.0
 speed auto
 duplex auto
!
router rip
 version 2
 no auto-summary
 !
 address-family ipv4 vrf VPN1
  network 10.0.0.0
  no auto-summary
```

```
 exit-address-family
 !
```

```
R4#sh run
 !
hostname R4
 !
vrf definition VPN1
 rd 1:1
 route-target export 1:1
 route-target import 1:1
 !
 address-family ipv4
 exit-address-family
 !
interface Loopback0
 ip address 4.4.4.4 255.255.255.0
 !
interface FastEthernet0/0
 vrf forwarding VPN1
 ip address 10.20.20.4 255.255.255.0
 speed auto
 duplex auto
 !
interface FastEthernet0/1
 ip address 10.0.34.4 255.255.255.0
 speed auto
 duplex auto
 !
router ospf 10 vrf VPN1
   network 10.20.20.4 0.0.0.0 area 10
 !
```

```
R5#show run
 !
hostname R5
 !
interface Loopback105
 ip address 10.5.5.5 255.255.255.0
 !
interface FastEthernet0/0
 ip address 10.10.10.5 255.255.255.0
 speed auto
 duplex auto
 !
router rip
 version 2
 network 10.0.0.0
 no auto-summary
 !
```

```
R6#show run
 !
hostname R6
 !
interface Loopback106
 ip address 10.6.6.6 255.255.255.0
 ip ospf network point-to-point
 !
interface FastEthernet0/0
```

```
 speed auto
 duplex auto
 !
router ospf 1
 network 10.0.0.0 0.255.255.255 area 10
 !
```

Core Configuration

- Configure OSPF 1 on R1, R2, R3 and R4 interconnections as area 0
- Inject Loopback 0 on R1 and R4 into OSPF area 0
- Configure an iBGP relationship between R1 and R4 using Loopback 0 as their sources

Again, this is based on the same configuration as number 3, so you could have saved this from the previous exercise.

```
R1#show run
!
hostname R1
!
interface Loopback0
 ip address 1.1.1.1 255.255.255.0
 ip ospf network point-to-point
 !
router ospf 1
 network 1.1.1.1 0.0.0.0 area 0
 network 10.0.0.0 0.255.255.255 area 0
 !
router bgp 65001
 bgp log-neighbor-changes
 neighbor 4.4.4.4 remote-as 65001
 neighbor 4.4.4.4 update-source Loopback0
 !
```

```
R2#show run
!
hostname R2
!
interface FastEthernet0/0
 ip address 10.0.23.2 255.255.255.0
 speed auto
 duplex auto
 !
interface FastEthernet0/1
 ip address 10.0.12.2 255.255.255.0
 speed auto
 duplex auto
 !
router ospf 1
 network 10.0.0.0 0.255.255.255 area 0
 !
```

```
R3#show run
!
hostname R3
!
interface FastEthernet0/0
 ip address 10.0.23.3 255.255.255.0
 speed auto
 duplex auto
```

```
!
interface FastEthernet0/1
 ip address 10.0.34.3 255.255.255.0
 speed auto
 duplex auto
!
router ospf 1
 network 10.0.0.0 0.255.255.255 area 0
!
```

```
R4#show run
!
hostname R4
!
interface Loopback0
 ip address 4.4.4.4 255.255.255.0
!
router ospf 1
 network 4.4.4.4 0.0.0.0 area 0
 network 10.0.0.0 0.255.255.255 area 0
!
router bgp 65001
 bgp log-neighbor-changes
 neighbor 1.1.1.1 remote-as 65001
 neighbor 1.1.1.1 update-source Loopback0
!
```

MPLS Configuration

- Enable MPLS on R1, R2, R3 and R4 interconnections
- Do not use multicast to discover LDP peers.
- Make sure that R2 advertises a label of 1110 for 1.1.1.0/24 and R3 advertises a label of 4440 for 4.4.4.0/24.

This is where things start to get a little different from the previous exercise. We are still running MPLS on the same set of routers, but we are not allowed to use multicast to discover neighbors...which means unicast or targeted neighbor statements. Also, we are told to use specific labels for a couple routes from R2 and R3, which is using static label assignments.

```
R1#sh run
!
hostname R1
!
mpls ldp neighbor 10.0.23.2 targeted ldp
!
interface FastEthernet0/1
 ip address 10.0.12.1 255.255.255.0
 speed auto
 duplex auto
 mpls ip
!
router rip
 version 2
 no auto-summary
 !
 address-family ipv4 vrf VPN1
  redistribute bgp 65001 metric 2
  network 10.0.0.0
```

```
  no auto-summary
 exit-address-family
!
router bgp 65001
 bgp log-neighbor-changes
 neighbor 4.4.4.4 remote-as 65001
 neighbor 4.4.4.4 update-source Loopback0
 !
 address-family vpnv4
  neighbor 4.4.4.4 activate
  neighbor 4.4.4.4 send-community extended
 exit-address-family
 !
 address-family ipv4 vrf VPN1
  redistribute rip
 exit-address-family
!
```
```
R2#show run
!
hostname R2
!
mpls label range 16 1109 static 1110 1110
mpls ldp neighbor 1.1.1.1 targeted ldp
mpls ldp neighbor 10.0.34.3 targeted ldp
!
interface FastEthernet0/0
 ip address 10.0.23.2 255.255.255.0
 speed auto
 duplex auto
 mpls ip
!
interface FastEthernet0/1
 ip address 10.0.12.2 255.255.255.0
 speed auto
 duplex auto
 mpls ip
!
mpls static binding ipv4 1.1.1.0 255.255.255.0 1110
!
```
```
R3#show run
!
hostname R3
!
mpls label range 16 4439 static 4440 4440
mpls ldp neighbor 10.0.23.2 targeted ldp
mpls ldp neighbor 4.4.4.4 targeted ldp
!
interface FastEthernet0/0
 ip address 10.0.23.3 255.255.255.0
 speed auto
 duplex auto
 mpls ip
!
interface FastEthernet0/1
 ip address 10.0.34.3 255.255.255.0
 speed auto
 duplex auto
 mpls ip
```

```
mpls static binding ipv4 4.4.4.0 255.255.255.0 4440
!
```

```
R4#show run
!
hostname R4
!
mpls ldp neighbor 10.0.34.3 targeted ldp
!
interface FastEthernet0/1
 ip address 10.0.34.4 255.255.255.0
 speed auto
 duplex auto
 mpls ip
!
router ospf 10 vrf VPN1
 redistribute bgp 65001 subnets
 network 10.20.20.4 0.0.0.0 area 10
!
router bgp 65001
 bgp log-neighbor-changes
 neighbor 1.1.1.1 remote-as 65001
 neighbor 1.1.1.1 update-source Loopback0
 !
 address-family vpnv4
  neighbor 1.1.1.1 activate
  neighbor 1.1.1.1 send-community extended
 exit-address-family
 !
 address-family ipv4 vrf VPN1
  redistribute ospf 10
 exit-address-family
!
```

We can see from the output of the debug that the destination is a unicast (1.1.1.1 in this case), not the multicast of 224.0.0.2. LDP uses UDP port number 646.

```
R1# deb ip pack det
IP packet debugging is on (detailed)
*May 16 12:08:58.726: IP: s=10.0.23.2 (FastEthernet0/1), d=1.1.1.1,
len 62, input feature
*May 16 12:08:58.730:    UDP src=646, dst=646
R1#, MCI Check(85), rtype 0, forus FALSE, sendself FALSE, mtu 0,
fwdchk FALSE
```

From the output of the LFIB you can see that R2 has a local label of 1110 for 1.1.1.0/24 and a learned label of 4440 for 4.4.4.0/24 from R3.

```
R2# show mpls forwarding-table
Local      Outgoing    Prefix          Bytes Label  Outgoing   Next
Hop
Label      Label    or Tunnel Id    Switched     interface
18         Pop Label   10.0.34.0/24        0                    Fa0/0
10.0.23.3
19         4440        4.4.4.0/24        2749                   Fa0/0
10.0.23.3
1110       Pop Label   1.1.1.0/24       22680                   Fa0/1
```

```
10.0.12.1
R2#show mpls ip binding
  1.1.1.0/24
        in label:     1110
        out label:    imp-null  lsr: 1.1.1.1:0
        out label:    16        lsr: 10.0.34.3:0
  4.4.4.0/24
        in label:     19
        out label:    21        lsr: 1.1.1.1:0
        out label:    4440      lsr: 10.0.34.3:0
  10.0.12.0/24
        in label:     imp-null
        out label:    imp-null  lsr: 1.1.1.1:0
        out label:    18        lsr: 10.0.34.3:0
  10.0.23.0/24
        in label:     imp-null
        out label:    17        lsr: 1.1.1.1:0
        out label:    imp-null  lsr: 10.0.34.3:0
  10.0.34.0/24
        in label:     18
        out label:    18        lsr: 1.1.1.1:0
        out label:    imp-null  lsr: 10.0.34.3:0
```

Make sure that R5 and R6 can ping others Loopback interfaces.

```
R5#sh ip route
Codes: L - local, C - connected, S - static, R - RIP, M - mobile, B -
BGP
       D - EIGRP, EX - EIGRP external, O - OSPF, IA - OSPF inter area
       N1 - OSPF NSSA external type 1, N2 - OSPF NSSA external type 2
       E1 - OSPF external type 1, E2 - OSPF external type 2
       i - IS-IS, su - IS-IS summary, L1 - IS-IS level-1, L2 - IS-IS
level-2
       ia - IS-IS inter area, * - candidate default, U - per-user
static route
       o - ODR, P - periodic downloaded static route, H - NHRP, l -
LISP
       + - replicated route, % - next hop override

Gateway of last resort is not set

      10.0.0.0/8 is variably subnetted, 6 subnets, 2 masks
C        10.5.5.0/24 is directly connected, Loopback105
L        10.5.5.5/32 is directly connected, Loopback105
R              10.6.6.6/32 [120/2] via  10.10.10.1,  00:00:08,
FastEthernet0/0
C        10.10.10.0/24 is directly connected, FastEthernet0/0
L        10.10.10.5/32 is directly connected, FastEthernet0/0
R              10.20.20.0/24 [120/2] via  10.10.10.1,  00:00:08,
FastEthernet0/0
R6#show ip route
Codes: L - local, C - connected, S - static, R - RIP, M - mobile, B -
BGP
       D - EIGRP, EX - EIGRP external, O - OSPF, IA - OSPF inter area
       N1 - OSPF NSSA external type 1, N2 - OSPF NSSA external type 2
       E1 - OSPF external type 1, E2 - OSPF external type 2
       i - IS-IS, su - IS-IS summary, L1 - IS-IS level-1, L2 - IS-IS
level-2
       ia - IS-IS inter area, * - candidate default, U - per-user
static route
```

```
          o - ODR, P - periodic downloaded static route, H - NHRP, l -
LISP
          + - replicated route, % - next hop override

Gateway of last resort is not set

       10.0.0.0/8 is variably subnetted, 6 subnets, 2 masks
O    E2           10.5.5.0/24   [110/1]  via  10.20.20.4,   00:10:54,
FastEthernet0/0
C        10.6.6.0/24 is directly connected, Loopback106
L        10.6.6.6/32 is directly connected, Loopback106
O    E2           10.10.10.0/24  [110/1]  via  10.20.20.4,   00:10:54,
FastEthernet0/0
C        10.20.20.0/24 is directly connected, FastEthernet0/0
L        10.20.20.6/32 is directly connected, FastEthernet0/0
```
```
R5#ping 10.6.6.6 sou lo 105
Type escape sequence to abort.
Sending 5, 100-byte ICMP Echos to 10.6.6.6, timeout is 2 seconds:
Packet sent with a source address of 10.5.5.5
!!!!!
Success   rate  is  100  percent  (5/5),  round-trip  min/avg/max  =
116/145/176 ms
```

Here are all the configs for the routers involved:

```
R1#sh run
!
hostname R1
!
vrf definition VPN1
 rd 1:1
 route-target export 1:1
 route-target import 1:1
 !
 address-family ipv4
 exit-address-family
!
mpls ldp neighbor 10.0.23.2 targeted ldp
!
interface Loopback0
 ip address 1.1.1.1 255.255.255.0
 ip ospf network point-to-point
!
interface FastEthernet0/0
 vrf forwarding VPN1
 ip address 10.10.10.1 255.255.255.0
 speed auto
 duplex auto
!
interface FastEthernet0/1
 ip address 10.0.12.1 255.255.255.0
 speed auto
 duplex auto
 mpls ip
!
router ospf 1
 network 1.1.1.1 0.0.0.0 area 0
 network 10.0.0.0 0.255.255.255 area 0
!
router rip
```

```
 version 2
 no auto-summary
 !
 address-family ipv4 vrf VPN1
  redistribute bgp 65001 metric 2
  network 10.0.0.0
  no auto-summary
 exit-address-family
 !
 router bgp 65001
  bgp log-neighbor-changes
  neighbor 4.4.4.4 remote-as 65001
  neighbor 4.4.4.4 update-source Loopback0
  !
  address-family vpnv4
   neighbor 4.4.4.4 activate
   neighbor 4.4.4.4 send-community extended
  exit-address-family
  !
  address-family ipv4 vrf VPN1
   redistribute rip
  exit-address-family
 !
```

```
R2#show run
!
hostname R2
!
mpls label range 16 1109 static 1110 1110
mpls ldp neighbor 1.1.1.1 targeted ldp
mpls ldp neighbor 10.0.34.3 targeted ldp
!
interface FastEthernet0/0
 ip address 10.0.23.2 255.255.255.0
 speed auto
 duplex auto
 mpls ip
!
interface FastEthernet0/1
 ip address 10.0.12.2 255.255.255.0
 speed auto
 duplex auto
 mpls ip
!
router ospf 1
 network 10.0.0.0 0.255.255.255 area 0
!
mpls static binding ipv4 1.1.1.0 255.255.255.0 1110
!
```

```
R3#show run
!
hostname R3
!
mpls label range 16 4439 static 4440 4440
mpls ldp neighbor 10.0.23.2 targeted ldp
mpls ldp neighbor 4.4.4.4 targeted ldp
!
interface FastEthernet0/0
 ip address 10.0.23.3 255.255.255.0
```

```
 speed auto
 duplex auto
 mpls ip
!
interface FastEthernet0/1
 ip address 10.0.34.3 255.255.255.0
 speed auto
 duplex auto
 mpls ip
!
router ospf 1
 network 10.0.0.0 0.255.255.255 area 0
!
mpls static binding ipv4 4.4.4.0 255.255.255.0 4440
!
```
```
R4#show run
!
hostname R4
!
vrf definition VPN1
 rd 1:1
 route-target export 1:1
 route-target import 1:1
 !
 address-family ipv4
 exit-address-family
!
mpls ldp neighbor 10.0.34.3 targeted ldp
!
interface Loopback0
 ip address 4.4.4.4 255.255.255.0
 ip ospf network point-to-point
!
interface FastEthernet0/0
 vrf forwarding VPN1
 ip address 10.20.20.4 255.255.255.0
 speed auto
 duplex auto
!
interface FastEthernet0/1
 ip address 10.0.34.4 255.255.255.0
 speed auto
 duplex auto
 mpls ip
!
router ospf 10 vrf VPN1
 redistribute bgp 65001 subnets
 network 10.20.20.4 0.0.0.0 area 10
!
router ospf 1
 network 4.4.4.4 0.0.0.0 area 0
 network 10.0.0.0 0.255.255.255 area 0
!
router bgp 65001
 bgp log-neighbor-changes
 neighbor 1.1.1.1 remote-as 65001
 neighbor 1.1.1.1 update-source Loopback0
 !
 address-family ipv4
```

```
  neighbor 1.1.1.1 activate
  neighbor 1.1.1.1 send-community extended
 exit-address-family
 !
 address-family ipv4 vrf VPN1
  redistribute ospf 10
 exit-address-family
 !
```
```
R5#show run
 !
 hostname R5
 !
 interface Loopback105
  ip address 10.5.5.5 255.255.255.0
 !
 interface FastEthernet0/0
  ip address 10.10.10.5 255.255.255.0
  speed auto
  duplex auto
 !
 router rip
  version 2
  network 10.0.0.0
  no auto-summary
 !
```
```
R6#show run
 !
 hostname R6
 !
 interface Loopback106
  ip address 10.6.6.6 255.255.255.0
 !
 interface FastEthernet0/0
  ip address 10.20.20.6 255.255.255.0
  speed auto
  duplex auto
 !
 router ospf 1
  network 10.0.0.0 0.255.255.255 area 10
 !
```

5)

This is a modification of the topology from exercise 3 and 4. First, the CE to PE protocol is now BGP. I've also added another devices into the mix, but it's not part of any VRF. This is going to require route leaking on R1 so that SW1 will be able to speak to R5. The reset of the foundation and core configuration doesn't change from the previous exercises.

- Configure the VLANs, trunking and port assignments based on the diagram, make sure to trunk to R1 FastEthernet0/0.

```
SW1-SW# sh run
!
hostname SW1-SW
!
vtp domain ccie
vtp mode transparent
vlan 10,15,23,46
!
interface FastEthernet1/1
 switchport mode trunk
 duplex full
 speed 100
!
interface FastEthernet1/2
 switchport access vlan 23
 duplex full
 speed 100
!
interface FastEthernet1/3
 switchport access vlan 23
 duplex full
 speed 100
!
interface FastEthernet1/4
 switchport access vlan 46
 duplex full
 speed 100
!
interface FastEthernet1/5
 switchport access vlan 15
 duplex full
 speed 100
!
interface FastEthernet1/6
 switchport access vlan 46
 duplex full
 speed 100
!
SW2-SW# sh run
!
```

```
hostname SW2-SW
!
vtp domain ccie
vtp mode transparent
vlan 12,34
!
interface FastEthernet1/1
 switchport access vlan 12
 duplex full
 speed 100
!
interface FastEthernet1/2
 switchport access vlan 12
 duplex full
 speed 100
!
interface FastEthernet1/3
 switchport access vlan 34
 duplex full
 speed 100
!
interface FastEthernet1/4
 switchport access vlan 34
 duplex full
 speed 100
```

- Place the interfaces feeding to R5 and R6 in a VRF instance name VPN1 on R1 and R4, respectively.
- Configure BGP between R5 and R1 on VLAN 15 and between R6 and R4 on VLAN 46.
- SW1 should have R1 as its default gateway, you are allowed to configure a static route for this on SW1.
- R1 FastEthernet0/0.10 is not in any VRF.

```
R1#show run
!
hostname R1
!
vrf definition VPN1
 rd 1:1
 route-target export 1:1
 route-target import 1:1
 !
 address-family ipv4
 exit-address-family
!
interface FastEthernet0/0
 no ip address
 speed auto
 duplex auto
!
interface FastEthernet0/0.10
 encapsulation dot1Q 10
 ip address 10.100.100.1 255.255.255.0
!
interface FastEthernet0/0.15
 encapsulation dot1Q 15
 vrf forwarding VPN1
```

```
  ip address 10.10.10.1 255.255.255.0
 !
 router bgp 65001
  bgp log-neighbor-changes
 !
 address-family ipv4 vrf VPN1
   neighbor 10.10.10.5 remote-as 65065
   neighbor 10.10.10.5 activate
   neighbor 10.10.10.5 as-override
  exit-address-family
 !
```

```
R4# show run
 !
 hostname R4
 !
 vrf definition VPN1
  rd 1:1
  route-target export 1:1
  route-target import 1:1
  !
  address-family ipv4
  exit-address-family
 !
 interface FastEthernet0/0
  vrf forwarding VPN1
  ip address 10.20.20.4 255.255.255.0
  speed auto
  duplex auto
 !
 router bgp 65001
  bgp log-neighbor-changes
 !
 address-family ipv4 vrf VPN1
   neighbor 10.20.20.6 remote-as 65065
   neighbor 10.20.20.6 activate
   neighbor 10.20.20.6 as-override
  exit-address-family
 !
```

```
R5#show run
 !
 hostname R5
 !
 interface Loopback105
  ip address 10.5.5.5 255.255.255.0
 !
 interface FastEthernet0/0
  ip address 10.10.10.5 255.255.255.0
  speed auto
  duplex auto
 !
 router bgp 65065
  bgp log-neighbor-changes
  network 10.5.5.0 mask 255.255.255.0
  neighbor 10.10.10.1 remote-as 65001
 !
```

```
R6# show run
 !
 hostname R6
```

```
interface Loopback106
 ip address 10.6.6.6 255.255.255.0
!
interface FastEthernet0/0
 ip address 10.20.20.6 255.255.255.0
 speed auto
 duplex auto
!
router bgp 65065
 bgp log-neighbor-changes
 network 10.6.6.0 mask 255.255.255.0
 neighbor 10.20.20.4 remote-as 65001
!
```

```
SW1-SW# sh run
!
hostname SW1-SW
!
interface Vlan10
 ip address 10.100.100.10 255.255.255.0
!
ip route 0.0.0.0 0.0.0.0 10.100.100.1
!
```

```
R5#show ip bgp summary
BGP router identifier 10.5.5.5, local AS number 65065
BGP table version is 5, main routing table version 5
1 network entries using 288 bytes of memory
12 path entries using 160 bytes of memory
1/1 BGP path/bestpath attribute entries using 272 bytes of memory
1 BGP AS-PATH entries using 24 bytes of memory
0 BGP route-map cache entries using 0 bytes of memory
0 BGP filter-list cache entries using 0 bytes of memory
BGP using 744 total bytes of memory
BGP activity 3/1 prefixes, 3/1 paths, scan interval 60 secs

Neighbor        V           AS MsgRcvd MsgSent   TblVer  InQ OutQ
Up/Down  State/PfxRcd
10.10.10.1      4        65001      16      14        5    0    0
00:08:58         0
```

```
R6#show ip bgp summary
BGP router identifier 10.6.6.6, local AS number 65065
BGP table version is 3, main routing table version 3
1 network entries using 288 bytes of memory
1 path entries using 160 bytes of memory
1/1 BGP path/bestpath attribute entries using 272 bytes of memory
1 BGP AS-PATH entries using 24 bytes of memory
0 BGP route-map cache entries using 0 bytes of memory
0 BGP filter-list cache entries using 0 bytes of memory
BGP using 744 total bytes of memory
BGP activity 2/0 prefixes, 2/0 paths, scan interval 60 secs

Neighbor        V           AS MsgRcvd MsgSent   TblVer  InQ OutQ
Up/Down  State/PfxRcd
10.20.20.4      4        65001      12      12        3    0    0
00:06:48         0
```

Core Configuration

- Configure OSPF 1 on R1, R2, R3 and R4 interconnections as area 0

- Inject Loopback 0 on R1 and R4 into OSPF area 0
- Configure an iBGP relationship between R1 and R4 using Loopback 0 as their sources

```
R1#show run
!
hostname R1
!
interface Loopback0
 ip address 1.1.1.1 255.255.255.0
 ip ospf network point-to-point
!
router ospf 1
 network 1.1.1.1 0.0.0.0 area 0
 network 10.0.0.0 0.255.255.255 area 0
!
router bgp 65001
 bgp log-neighbor-changes
 neighbor 4.4.4.4 remote-as 65001
 neighbor 4.4.4.4 update-source Loopback0
 !
 address-family vpnv4
  neighbor 4.4.4.4 activate
  neighbor 4.4.4.4 send-community extended
 exit-address-family
 !
 address-family ipv4 vrf VPN1
  neighbor 10.10.10.5 remote-as 65065
  neighbor 10.10.10.5 activate
  neighbor 10.10.10.5 as-override
 exit-address-family
!
```

```
R2#show run
!
hostname R2
!
interface FastEthernet0/0
 ip address 10.0.23.2 255.255.255.0
 speed auto
 duplex auto
!
interface FastEthernet0/1
 ip address 10.0.12.2 255.255.255.0
 speed auto
 duplex auto
!
router ospf 1
 network 10.0.0.0 0.255.255.255 area 0
!
```

```
R3#show run
!
hostname R3
!
interface FastEthernet0/0
 ip address 10.0.23.3 255.255.255.0
 speed auto
 duplex auto
!
```

```
 ip address 10.0.34.3 255.255.255.0
 speed auto
 duplex auto
!
router ospf 1
 network 10.0.0.0 0.255.255.255 area 0
!
```
```
R4#show run
!
hostname R4
!
interface Loopback0
 ip address 4.4.4.4 255.255.255.0
!
router ospf 1
 network 4.4.4.4 0.0.0.0 area 0
 network 10.0.0.0 0.255.255.255 area 0
!
router bgp 65001
 bgp log-neighbor-changes
 neighbor 1.1.1.1 remote-as 65001
 neighbor 1.1.1.1 update-source Loopback0
 !
 address-family vpnv4
  neighbor 1.1.1.1 activate
  neighbor 1.1.1.1 send-community extended
 exit-address-family
 !
 address-family ipv4 vrf VPN1
  neighbor 10.20.20.6 remote-as 65065
  neighbor 10.20.20.6 activate
  neighbor 10.20.20.6 as-override
 exit-address-family
!
```

MPLS Configuration

- Enable MPLS on R1, R2, R3 and R4 interconnections
- Configure R1 such that SW1 will be able to speak to R5 and R6

The second bullet here is the interesting one, route leaking from the VRF to the global routing table and back again.

```
R1#show run
!
hostname R1
!
!
interface FastEthernet0/1
 ip address 10.0.12.1 255.255.255.0
 speed auto
 duplex auto
 mpls ip
!
router bgp 65001
 bgp log-neighbor-changes
 neighbor 4.4.4.4 remote-as 65001
 neighbor 4.4.4.4 update-source Loopback0
 !
```

```
  neighbor 4.4.4.4 activate
  neighbor 4.4.4.4 send-community extended
 exit-address-family
 !
 address-family ipv4 vrf VPN1
  redistribute static
  neighbor 10.10.10.5 remote-as 65065
  neighbor 10.10.10.5 activate
  neighbor 10.10.10.5 as-override
 exit-address-family
 !
 ! the first two static routes adds the routes to the global routing
 table to reach the IPv4 address of R5
 ip route 10.5.5.0 255.255.255.0 FastEthernet0/0.15
 ip route 10.10.10.0 255.255.255.0 FastEthernet0/0.15
 ! the next static routes add the return to SW1 in the VRF to feed to
 R5.  Note above that redistribute
 ! static was added under the address family for VRF VPN1.
 ip  route  vrf  VPN1  10.100.100.0  255.255.255.0  FastEthernet0/0.10
 10.100.100.10
 !
```

```
R2#show run
 !
 hostname R2
 !
 interface FastEthernet0/0
  ip address 10.0.23.2 255.255.255.0
  speed auto
  duplex auto
  mpls ip
 !
 interface FastEthernet0/1
  ip address 10.0.12.2 255.255.255.0
  speed auto
  duplex auto
  mpls ip
 !
```

```
R3#show run
 !
 hostname R3
 !
 interface FastEthernet0/0
  ip address 10.0.23.3 255.255.255.0
  speed auto
  duplex auto
  mpls ip
 !
 interface FastEthernet0/1
  ip address 10.0.34.3 255.255.255.0
  speed auto
  duplex auto
  mpls ip
 !
```

```
R4#show run
 !
 hostname R4
 !
 mpls ldp password required
```

```
mpls ldp explicit-null
!
interface FastEthernet0/1
 ip address 10.0.34.4 255.255.255.0
 speed auto
 duplex auto
 mpls ip
!
router bgp 65001
 bgp log-neighbor-changes
 neighbor 1.1.1.1 remote-as 65001
 neighbor 1.1.1.1 update-source Loopback0
 !
 address-family vpnv4
  neighbor 1.1.1.1 activate
  neighbor 1.1.1.1 send-community extended
 exit-address-family
 !
 address-family ipv4 vrf VPN1
  redistribute ospf 10
 exit-address-family
!
```

```
R5#show ip bgp
BGP table version is 6, local router ID is 10.5.5.5
Status codes: s suppressed, d damped, h history, * valid, > best, i -
internal,
              r RIB-failure, S Stale, m multipath, b backup-path, f
RT-Filter,
              x best-external, a additional-path, c RIB-compressed,
Origin codes: i - IGP, e - EGP, ? - incomplete
RPKI validation codes: V valid, I invalid, N Not found

     Network          Next Hop          Metric LocPrf Weight Path
 *>  10.5.5.0/24      0.0.0.0                0          32768 i
 *>  10.6.6.0/24      10.10.10.1                            0 65001
65001 i
 *>  10.100.100.0/24  10.10.10.1             0              0 65001
?
R5#
```

Make sure that R5 can ping SW1.

```
R5#p 10.100.100.10
Type escape sequence to abort.
Sending  5,  100-byte  ICMP  Echos  to  10.100.100.10,  timeout  is  2
seconds:
!!!!!
Success rate is 100 percent (5/5), round-trip min/avg/max = 60/80/128
ms
```

```
R5#ping 10.100.100.10 source loop 105
Type escape sequence to abort.
Sending  5,  100-byte  ICMP  Echos  to  10.100.100.10,  timeout  is  2
seconds:
Packet sent with a source address of 10.5.5.5
!!!!!
Success  rate  is  100  percent  (5/5),  round-trip  min/avg/max  =
52/117/260 ms
R5#
```

```
R5#ping 10.6.6.6 source loop 105
Type escape sequence to abort.
```

```
Sending 5, 100-byte ICMP Echos to 10.6.6.6, timeout is 2 seconds:
Packet sent with a source address of 10.5.5.5
!!!!!
Success   rate   is   100   percent   (5/5),   round-trip   min/avg/max   =
144/168/212 ms
R5#
```

Here are the configs for the routers involved:

```
R1#sh run
!
hostname R1
!
vrf definition VPN1
 rd 1:1
 route-target export 1:1
 route-target import 1:1
 !
 address-family ipv4
 exit-address-family
!
interface Loopback0
 ip address 1.1.1.1 255.255.255.0
 ip ospf network point-to-point
!
interface FastEthernet0/0
 no ip address
 speed auto
 duplex auto
!
interface FastEthernet0/0.10
 encapsulation dot1Q 10
 ip address 10.100.100.1 255.255.255.0
!
interface FastEthernet0/0.15
 encapsulation dot1Q 15
 vrf forwarding VPN1
 ip address 10.10.10.1 255.255.255.0
!
interface FastEthernet0/1
 ip address 10.0.12.1 255.255.255.0
 speed auto
 duplex auto
 mpls ip
!
router ospf 1
 network 1.1.1.1 0.0.0.0 area 0
 network 10.0.0.0 0.255.255.255 area 0
!
router bgp 65001
 bgp log-neighbor-changes
 neighbor 4.4.4.4 remote-as 65001
 neighbor 4.4.4.4 update-source Loopback0
 !
 address-family vpnv4
  neighbor 4.4.4.4 activate
  neighbor 4.4.4.4 send-community extended
 exit-address-family
 !
 address-family ipv4 vrf VPN1
```

```
    redistribute static
    neighbor 10.10.10.5 remote-as 65065
    neighbor 10.10.10.5 activate
    neighbor 10.10.10.5 as-override
  exit-address-family
 !
ip route 10.5.5.0 255.255.255.0 FastEthernet0/0.15
ip route 10.10.10.0 255.255.255.0 FastEthernet0/0.15
ip  route  vrf  VPN1  10.100.100.0  255.255.255.0  FastEthernet0/0.10
10.100.100.10
 !
```

```
R2#show run
 !
hostname R2
 !
interface FastEthernet0/0
 ip address 10.0.23.2 255.255.255.0
 speed auto
 duplex auto
 mpls ip
 !
interface FastEthernet0/1
 ip address 10.0.12.2 255.255.255.0
 speed auto
 duplex auto
 mpls ip
 !
router ospf 1
 network 10.0.0.0 0.255.255.255 area 0
 !
```

```
R3#show run
 !
hostname R3
 !
interface FastEthernet0/0
 ip address 10.0.23.3 255.255.255.0
 speed auto
 duplex auto
 mpls ip
 !
interface FastEthernet0/1
 ip address 10.0.34.3 255.255.255.0
 speed auto
 duplex auto
 mpls ip
 !
router ospf 1
 network 10.0.0.0 0.255.255.255 area 0
 !
```

```
R4#show run
 !
hostname R4
 !
vrf definition VPN1
 rd 1:1
 route-target export 1:1
 route-target import 1:1
 !
```

```
  exit-address-family
 !
interface Loopback0
 ip address 4.4.4.4 255.255.255.0
 ip ospf network point-to-point
 !
interface FastEthernet0/0
 vrf forwarding VPN1
 ip address 10.20.20.4 255.255.255.0
 speed auto
 duplex auto
 !
interface FastEthernet0/1
 ip address 10.0.34.4 255.255.255.0
 speed auto
 duplex auto
 mpls ip
 !
router ospf 1
 network 4.4.4.4 0.0.0.0 area 0
 network 10.0.0.0 0.255.255.255 area 0
 !
router bgp 65001
 bgp log-neighbor-changes
 neighbor 1.1.1.1 remote-as 65001
 neighbor 1.1.1.1 update-source Loopback0
 !
 address-family vpnv4
  neighbor 1.1.1.1 activate
  neighbor 1.1.1.1 send-community extended
 exit-address-family
 !
 address-family ipv4 vrf VPN1
  neighbor 10.20.20.6 remote-as 65065
  neighbor 10.20.20.6 activate
  neighbor 10.20.20.6 as-override
 exit-address-family
 !
R5#show run
 !
hostname R5
 !
interface Loopback105
 ip address 10.5.5.5 255.255.255.0
 !
interface FastEthernet0/0
 ip address 10.10.10.5 255.255.255.0
 speed auto
 duplex auto
 !
router bgp 65065
 bgp log-neighbor-changes
 network 10.5.5.0 mask 255.255.255.0
 neighbor 10.10.10.1 remote-as 65001
 !
R6#show run
 !
hostname R6
```

-

```
interface Loopback106
 ip address 10.6.6.6 255.255.255.0
!
interface FastEthernet0/0
 ip address 10.20.20.6 255.255.255.0
 speed auto
 duplex auto
!
router bgp 65065
 bgp log-neighbor-changes
 network 10.6.6.0 mask 255.255.255.0
 neighbor 10.20.20.4 remote-as 65001
!
```

```
SW1-SW#show run
!
hostname SW1-SW
!
vtp domain ccie
vtp mode transparent
!
vlan 10,15,23,46
!
interface FastEthernet1/1
 switchport mode trunk
 duplex full
 speed 100
!
interface FastEthernet1/2
 switchport access vlan 23
 duplex full
 speed 100
!
interface FastEthernet1/3
 switchport access vlan 23
 duplex full
 speed 100
!
interface FastEthernet1/4
 switchport access vlan 46
 duplex full
 speed 100
!
interface FastEthernet1/5
 switchport access vlan 15
 duplex full
 speed 100
!
interface FastEthernet1/6
 switchport access vlan 46
 duplex full
 speed 100
!
interface Vlan10
 ip address 10.100.100.10 255.255.255.0
!
ip route 0.0.0.0 0.0.0.0 10.100.100.1
!
```

```
SW2-SW#show run
```

```
hostname SW2-SW
!
no ip routing
!
vtp domain ccie
vtp mode transparent
!
vlan 12,34
!
interface FastEthernet1/1
 switchport access vlan 12
 duplex full
 speed 100
!
interface FastEthernet1/2
 switchport access vlan 12
 duplex full
 speed 100
!
interface FastEthernet1/3
 switchport access vlan 34
 duplex full
 speed 100
!
interface FastEthernet1/4
 switchport access vlan 34
 duplex full
 speed 100
!
```

6)

This exercise has a little of a twist in it, in that the PE routers are not going to be peering with each other using BGP. We have to configure a route reflector. This exercise also has you configure a sham link to satisfy one of the requirements.

- Configure the VLANs, trunking and port assignments based on the diagram.
- Place the interfaces feeding to R5 and R6 in a VRF instance name VPN1 on R1 and R4, respectively.
- Configure OSPF Area 10 between R5 and R1 on VLAN 15 and between R6 and R4 on VLAN 46.

This is similar the previous few exercises, but the CE to PE routing protocol is OSPF.

```
SW1-SW#sh run
!
hostname SW1-SW
!
vtp domain ccie
vtp mode transparent
!
vlan 10,15,23,46
```

```
interface FastEthernet1/1
 switchport access vlan 15
 duplex full
 speed 100
!
interface FastEthernet1/2
 switchport access vlan 23
 duplex full
 speed 100
!
interface FastEthernet1/3
 switchport access vlan 23
!
interface FastEthernet1/4
 switchport access vlan 46
!
interface FastEthernet1/5
 switchport access vlan 15
!
interface FastEthernet1/6
 switchport access vlan 46
!
```
```
SW2-SW#sh run
!
hostname SW2-SW
!
vtp domain ccie
vtp mode transparent
!
vlan 12,34
!
interface FastEthernet1/1
 switchport access vlan 12
!
interface FastEthernet1/2
 switchport access vlan 12
!
interface FastEthernet1/3
 switchport access vlan 34
!
interface FastEthernet1/4
 switchport access vlan 34
!
interface FastEthernet1/5
 switchport access vlan 25
!
```
```
R1# sh run
!
hostname R1
!
vrf definition VPN1
 rd 1:1
 route-target export 1:1
 route-target import 1:1
 !
 address-family ipv4
 exit-address-family
 interface FastEthernet0/0
```

```
  vrf forwarding VPN1
  ip address 10.10.10.1 255.255.255.0
 !
 router ospf 2 vrf VPN1
  network 10.0.0.0 0.255.255.255 area 10
 !
```

```
R4#show run
 !
 hostname R4
 !
 vrf definition VPN1
  rd 1:1
  route-target export 1:1
  route-target import 1:1
  !
  address-family ipv4
  exit-address-family
 !
 interface FastEthernet0/0
  vrf forwarding VPN1
  ip address 10.20.20.4 255.255.255.0
 !
 router ospf 2 vrf VPN1
  network 10.0.0.0 0.255.255.255 area 10
 !
```

```
R5#show run
 !
 hostname R5
 !
 !
 interface Loopback105
  ip address 10.5.5.5 255.255.255.0
  ip ospf network point-to-point
 !
 interface FastEthernet0/0
  ip address 10.10.10.5 255.255.255.0
 !
 router ospf 1
  network 10.0.0.0 0.255.255.255 area 10
 !
```

```
R6#show run
 !
 hostname R6
 !
 interface Loopback106
  ip address 10.6.6.6 255.255.255.0
  ip ospf network point-to-point
 !
 interface FastEthernet0/0
  ip address 10.20.20.6 255.255.255.0
 !
 router ospf 1
  network 10.0.0.0 0.255.255.255 area 10
 !
```

```
R5#show ip ospf neighbor

Neighbor ID      Pri     State              Dead Time      Address
Interface
```

```
FastEthernet0/0
R6#show ip ospf nei

Neighbor ID        Pri    State            Dead  Time     Address
Interface
10.20.20.4          1     FULL/DR          00:00:32      10.20.20.4
FastEthernet0/0
```
```
R1#show ip route vrf VPN1

Routing Table: VPN1
Codes: L - local, C - connected, S - static, R - RIP, M - mobile, B -
BGP
       D - EIGRP, EX - EIGRP external, O - OSPF, IA - OSPF inter area
       N1 - OSPF NSSA external type 1, N2 - OSPF NSSA external type 2
       E1 - OSPF external type 1, E2 - OSPF external type 2
       i - IS-IS, su - IS-IS summary, L1 - IS-IS level-1, L2 - IS-IS
level-2
       ia - IS-IS inter area, * - candidate default, U - per-user
static route
       o - ODR, P - periodic downloaded static route, H - NHRP, l -
LISP
       + - replicated route, % - next hop override

Gateway of last resort is not set

      10.0.0.0/8 is variably subnetted, 3 subnets, 2 masks
O              10.5.5.0/24   [110/2]  via  10.10.10.5,  00:01:05,
FastEthernet0/0
C       10.10.10.0/24 is directly connected, FastEthernet0/0
L       10.10.10.1/32 is directly connected, FastEthernet0/0
```

Core Configuration

- SW1 should have an SVI in VLAN23
- SW1 should not have any VRFs configured
- Configure OSPF 1 on R1, R2, R3,R4 and SW1 interconnections as area 0
- Inject Loopback 0 on R1, R4 and SW1 into OSPF area 0

```
SW1-SW#show run | b Loop
!
interface Loopback110
 ip address 10.110.110.10 255.255.255.0
 ip ospf network point-to-point
!
interface Vlan23
 ip address 10.0.23.10 255.255.255.0
!
router ospf 1
 log-adjacency-changes
 network 10.0.0.0 0.255.255.255 area 0
!
```
```
R1#show run | b Loop
!
interface Loopback0
 ip address 1.1.1.1 255.255.255.0
 ip ospf network point-to-point
!
interface FastEthernet0/1
```

```
!
router ospf 1
 network 1.1.1.1 0.0.0.0 area 0
 network 10.0.0.0 0.255.255.255 area 0
 !
R2#show run
 !
hostname R2
 !
interface FastEthernet0/0
 ip address 10.0.23.2 255.255.255.0
 !
interface FastEthernet0/1
 ip address 10.0.12.2 255.255.255.0
 !
router ospf 1
 network 10.0.0.0 0.255.255.255 area 0
 !
R3#show run
 !
hostname R3
 !
interface FastEthernet0/0
 ip address 10.0.23.3 255.255.255.0
 !
interface FastEthernet0/1
 ip address 10.0.34.3 255.255.255.0
 !
router ospf 1
 network 10.0.0.0 0.255.255.255 area 0
 !
R4#show run | b Loop
 !
interface Loopback0
 ip address 4.4.4.4 255.255.255.0
 ip ospf network point-to-point
 !
interface FastEthernet0/1
 ip address 10.0.34.4 255.255.255.0
 !
router ospf 1
 network 4.4.4.4 0.0.0.0 area 0
 network 10.0.0.0 0.255.255.255 area 0
 !
R1#show ip route
Codes: L - local, C - connected, S - static, R - RIP, M - mobile, B -
BGP
       D - EIGRP, EX - EIGRP external, O - OSPF, IA - OSPF inter area
       N1 - OSPF NSSA external type 1, N2 - OSPF NSSA external type 2
       E1 - OSPF external type 1, E2 - OSPF external type 2
       i - IS-IS, su - IS-IS summary, L1 - IS-IS level-1, L2 - IS-IS
level-2
       ia - IS-IS inter area, * - candidate default, U - per-user
static route
       o - ODR, P - periodic downloaded static route, H - NHRP, l -
LISP
       + - replicated route, % - next hop override
```

```
       1.0.0.0/8 is variably subnetted, 2 subnets, 2 masks
C         1.1.1.0/24 is directly connected, Loopback0
L         1.1.1.1/32 is directly connected, Loopback0
       4.0.0.0/24 is subnetted, 1 subnets
O         4.4.4.0 [110/4] via 10.0.12.2, 00:25:59, FastEthernet0/1
       10.0.0.0/8 is variably subnetted, 5 subnets, 2 masks
C         10.0.12.0/24 is directly connected, FastEthernet0/1
L         10.0.12.1/32 is directly connected, FastEthernet0/1
O                 10.0.23.0/24  [110/2]  via  10.0.12.2,  00:25:59,
FastEthernet0/1
O                 10.0.34.0/24  [110/3]  via  10.0.12.2,  00:25:59,
FastEthernet0/1
O         10.110.110.0/24  [110/3]  via  10.0.12.2,  00:08:26,
FastEthernet0/1
```

- Configure an iBGP relationships between R1 & SW1 and R4 & SW1 using Loopback 0 to SW1 Loopback 110 as their sources, do not form a relationship between R1 and R4

This is an interesting issue...we are not allowed to have a full mesh of iBGP peering relationships, which at first seems like no big deal, just configure SW1 as a route reflector.

```
R1#show run | s bgp
!
router bgp 65001
 bgp log-neighbor-changes
 neighbor 10.110.110.10 remote-as 65001
 neighbor 10.110.110.10 update-source Loopback0
```
```
R4#show run | s bgp
!
router bgp 65001
 bgp log-neighbor-changes
 neighbor 10.110.110.10 remote-as 65001
 neighbor 10.110.110.10 update-source Loopback0
```
```
SW1-SW#show run | s bgp
router bgp 65001
 no synchronization
 bgp log-neighbor-changes
 neighbor 1.1.1.1 remote-as 65001
 neighbor 1.1.1.1 update-source Loopback110
 neighbor 1.1.1.1 route-reflector-client
 neighbor 4.4.4.4 remote-as 65001
 neighbor 4.4.4.4 update-source Loopback110
 neighbor 4.4.4.4 route-reflector-client
 no auto-summary
```
```
SW1-SW#show ip bgp summary
BGP router identifier 10.110.110.10, local AS number 65001
BGP table version is 1, main routing table version 1

Neighbor      V     AS MsgRcvd MsgSent   TblVer   InQ OutQ Up/Down
State/PfxRcd
1.1.1.1       4 65001      15      13       1     0    0 00:05:32
0
4.4.4.4       4 65001      14      13       1     0    0 00:05:40
0
```
```
SW1-SW#show ip bgp neighbors 1.1.1.1
BGP neighbor is 1.1.1.1,  remote AS 65001, internal link
```

```
  BGP version 4, remote router ID 1.1.1.1
  BGP state = Established, up for 00:23:55
  Last read  00:00:02, last write  00:00:55, hold time  is  180,
keepalive interval is 60 seconds
  Neighbor capabilities:
    Route refresh: advertised and received(old & new)
    Address family IPv4 Unicast: advertised and received
  Message statistics:
    InQ depth is 0
    OutQ depth is 0
                        Sent          Rcvd
    Opens:                2             2
    Notifications:        0             0
    Updates:              0             2
    Keepalives:          29            31
    Route Refresh:        0             0
    Total:               31            35
  Default minimum time between advertisement runs is 0 seconds


 For address family: IPv4 Unicast
  BGP table version 1, neighbor version 1/0
  Output queue size: 0
  Index 2, Offset 0, Mask 0x4
  Route-Reflector Client
  2 update-group member
                          Sent          Rcvd
  Prefix activity:        ----          ----
    Prefixes Current:       0             0
    Prefixes Total:         0             0
    Implicit Withdraw:      0             0
    Explicit Withdraw:      0             0
    Used as bestpath:     n/a             0
    Used as multipath:    n/a             0
- output omitted -
```

MPLS Configuration

- Enable MPLS on R1, R2, R3, R4 and SW1 interconnections
- Pass the CE routes through the MPLS cloud as a Layer 3 VPN

Nothing too bad here, just apply the **mpls ip** command on all the related interfaces. But in the previous bullets they tell us not to configure VRFs on SW1, so how is the layer 3 VPN going to work?

```
SW1-SW#show run | b Vlan23
interface Vlan23
 ip address 10.0.23.10 255.255.255.0
 mpls ip
!
router ospf 1
 log-adjacency-changes
 network 10.0.0.0 0.255.255.255 area 0
!
router bgp 65001
 no synchronization
 bgp log-neighbor-changes
 neighbor 1.1.1.1 remote-as 65001
 neighbor 1.1.1.1 update-source Loopback110
 neighbor 1.1.1.1 route-reflector-client
```

```
  neighbor 4.4.4.4 remote-as 65001
  neighbor 4.4.4.4 update-source Loopback110
  neighbor 4.4.4.4 route-reflector-client
  no auto-summary
 !
```
```
R1#show run | b 0/1
interface FastEthernet0/1
 ip address 10.0.12.1 255.255.255.0
 mpls ip
!
router ospf 2 vrf VPN1
 redistribute bgp 65001 subnets
 network 10.0.0.0 0.255.255.255 area 10
!
router ospf 1
 network 1.1.1.1 0.0.0.0 area 0
 network 10.0.0.0 0.255.255.255 area 0
!
router bgp 65001
 bgp log-neighbor-changes
 neighbor 10.110.110.10 remote-as 65001
 neighbor 10.110.110.10 update-source Loopback0
 !
 address-family vpnv4
  neighbor 10.110.110.10 activate
  neighbor 10.110.110.10 send-community both
 exit-address-family
 !
 address-family ipv4 vrf VPN1
  redistribute ospf 2
 exit-address-family
!
```
```
R2#show run | b 0/0
interface FastEthernet0/0
 ip address 10.0.23.2 255.255.255.0
 mpls ip
!
interface FastEthernet0/1
 ip address 10.0.12.2 255.255.255.0
 mpls ip
!
```
```
R3#show run | b 0/0
interface FastEthernet0/0
 ip address 10.0.23.3 255.255.255.0
 mpls ip
!
interface FastEthernet0/1
 ip address 10.0.34.3 255.255.255.0
 mpls ip
!
```
```
R4#show run | b 0/1
interface FastEthernet0/1
 ip address 10.0.34.4 255.255.255.0
 mpls ip
!
router bgp 65001
 bgp log-neighbor-changes
 neighbor 10.110.110.10 remote-as 65001
```

```
!
address-family vpnv4
 neighbor 10.110.110.10 activate
 neighbor 10.110.110.10 send-community both
exit-address-family
!
address-family ipv4 vrf VPN1
 redistribute ospf 2
exit-address-family
!
```

```
SW1-SW#show mpls ldp neighbor
    Peer LDP Ident: 10.0.34.3:0; Local LDP Ident 10.110.110.10:0
        TCP connection: 10.0.34.3.646 - 10.110.110.10.18280
        State: Oper; Msgs sent/rcvd: 17/16; Downstream
        Up time: 00:06:40
        LDP discovery sources:
          Vlan23, Src IP addr: 10.0.23.3
        Addresses bound to peer LDP Ident:
          10.0.23.3        10.0.34.3
    Peer LDP Ident: 10.0.23.2:0; Local LDP Ident 10.110.110.10:0
        TCP connection: 10.0.23.2.646 - 10.110.110.10.36347
        State: Oper; Msgs sent/rcvd: 16/16; Downstream
        Up time: 00:06:40
        LDP discovery sources:
          Vlan23, Src IP addr: 10.0.23.2
        Addresses bound to peer LDP Ident:
          10.0.23.2        10.0.12.2
```

Hmmm, did it work? If we look at R1 or R4's BGP table related to the VRFs, we can see if it did:

```
R1#show ip bgp vpnv4 all
BGP table version is 3, local router ID is 1.1.1.1
Status codes: s suppressed, d damped, h history, * valid, > best, i -
internal,
              r RIB-failure, S Stale, m multipath, b backup-path, f
RT-Filter,
              x best-external, a additional-path, c RIB-compressed,
Origin codes: i - IGP, e - EGP, ? - incomplete
RPKI validation codes: V valid, I invalid, N Not found

     Network          Next Hop            Metric LocPrf Weight Path
Route Distinguisher: 1:1 (default for vrf VPN1)
 *>  10.5.5.0/24      10.10.10.5               2         32768 ?
 *>  10.10.10.0/24    0.0.0.0                  0         32768 ?
```

```
R4#show ip bgp vpnv4 all
BGP table version is 3, local router ID is 4.4.4.4
Status codes: s suppressed, d damped, h history, * valid, > best, i -
internal,
              r RIB-failure, S Stale, m multipath, b backup-path, f
RT-Filter,
              x best-external, a additional-path, c RIB-compressed,
Origin codes: i - IGP, e - EGP, ? - incomplete
RPKI validation codes: V valid, I invalid, N Not found

     Network          Next Hop            Metric LocPrf Weight Path
Route Distinguisher: 1:1 (default for vrf VPN1)
 *>  10.6.6.0/24      10.20.20.6               2         32768 ?
 *>  10.20.20.0/24    0.0.0.0                  0         32768 ?
```

Nope, doesn't look like SW1 is reflecting the routes for the VPNv4.

```
R1#sh ip bgp vpnv4 all neighbors 10.110.110.10 advertised-routes
BGP table version is 3, local router ID is 1.1.1.1
Status codes: s suppressed, d damped, h history, * valid, > best, i -
internal,
            r RIB-failure, S Stale, m multipath, b backup-path, f
RT-Filter,
            x best-external, a additional-path, c RIB-compressed,
Origin codes: i - IGP, e - EGP, ? - incomplete
RPKI validation codes: V valid, I invalid, N Not found

    Network          Next Hop          Metric LocPrf Weight Path
Route Distinguisher: 1:1 (default for vrf VPN1)
 *>  10.5.5.0/24      10.10.10.5             2          32768 ?
 *>  10.10.10.0/24    0.0.0.0                0          32768 ?

Total number of prefixes 2
```

We can see that R1 (and I would assume R4 as well) sent the routes, but does
SW1 have those routes?

```
SW1-SW#sh ip bgp
```

```
SW1-SW#sh ip bgp vpnv4 all
```

Nope! How do fix that you ask! We were not supposed to configure VRFs on
SW1, but the issue is that SW1 doesn't know how to deal with the routes since
they are associated to VPNv4. You need to add the R1 and R4 as neighbors under
the address family for VPNV4.

```
SW1-SW# sh run | b bgp
router bgp 65001
 no synchronization
 bgp log-neighbor-changes
 neighbor 1.1.1.1 remote-as 65001
 neighbor 1.1.1.1 update-source Loopback110
 neighbor 1.1.1.1 route-reflector-client
 neighbor 4.4.4.4 remote-as 65001
 neighbor 4.4.4.4 update-source Loopback110
 neighbor 4.4.4.4 route-reflector-client
 no auto-summary
 !
 address-family vpnv4
  neighbor 1.1.1.1 activate
  neighbor 1.1.1.1 send-community extended
  neighbor 4.4.4.4 activate
  neighbor 4.4.4.4 send-community extended
 exit-address-family
 !
SW1-SW#sh ip bgp vpnv4 all
```

Still nothing! The route reflector configuration is for IPv4 routes, not VPNv4
routes, you need to add R1 and R4 as route reflector clients (or just one of them)
under the address family VPNv4.

```
SW1-SW# sh run | b bgp
router bgp 65001
 no synchronization
 bgp log-neighbor-changes
 neighbor 1.1.1.1 remote-as 65001
```

```
 neighbor 1.1.1.1 update-source Loopback110
 neighbor 1.1.1.1 route-reflector-client
 neighbor 4.4.4.4 remote-as 65001
 neighbor 4.4.4.4 update-source Loopback110
 neighbor 4.4.4.4 route-reflector-client
 no auto-summary
 !
 address-family vpnv4
  neighbor 1.1.1.1 activate
  neighbor 1.1.1.1 send-community extended
  neighbor 1.1.1.1 route-reflector-client
  neighbor 4.4.4.4 activate
  neighbor 4.4.4.4 send-community extended
  neighbor 4.4.4.4 route-reflector-client
 exit-address-family
 !
```

```
SW1-SW#show ip bgp vpnv4 all
BGP table version is 15, local router ID is 10.110.110.10
Status codes: s suppressed, d damped, h history, * valid, > best, i -
internal,
              r RIB-failure, S Stale
Origin codes: i - IGP, e - EGP, ? - incomplete

   Network          Next Hop            Metric LocPrf Weight Path
Route Distinguisher: 1:1
*>i10.5.5.0/24      1.1.1.1                  2    100      0 ?
*>i10.6.6.0/24      4.4.4.4                  2    100      0 ?
*>i10.10.10.0/24    1.1.1.1                  0    100      0 ?
*>i10.20.20.0/24    4.4.4.4                  0    100      0 ?
```

```
R1#show ip bgp vpnv4 all
BGP table version is 49, local router ID is 1.1.1.1
Status codes: s suppressed, d damped, h history, * valid, > best, i -
internal,
              r RIB-failure, S Stale, m multipath, b backup-path, f
RT-Filter,
              x best-external, a additional-path, c RIB-compressed,
Origin codes: i - IGP, e - EGP, ? - incomplete
RPKI validation codes: V valid, I invalid, N Not found

    Network         Next Hop            Metric LocPrf Weight Path
Route Distinguisher: 1:1 (default for vrf VPN1)
 *>  10.5.5.0/24    10.10.10.5               2         32768 ?
 *>i 10.6.6.0/24    4.4.4.4                  2    100      0 ?
 *>  10.10.10.0/24  0.0.0.0                  0         32768 ?
 *>i 10.20.20.0/24  4.4.4.4                  0    100      0 ?
```

```
R5#show ip route
Codes: L - local, C - connected, S - static, R - RIP, M - mobile, B -
BGP
       D - EIGRP, EX - EIGRP external, O - OSPF, IA - OSPF inter area
       N1 - OSPF NSSA external type 1, N2 - OSPF NSSA external type 2
       E1 - OSPF external type 1, E2 - OSPF external type 2
       i - IS-IS, su - IS-IS summary, L1 - IS-IS level-1, L2 - IS-IS
level-2
       ia - IS-IS inter area, * - candidate default, U - per-user
static route
       o - ODR, P - periodic downloaded static route, H - NHRP, l -
LISP
       + - replicated route, % - next hop override
```

-

```
Gateway of last resort is not set

     10.0.0.0/8 is variably subnetted, 6 subnets, 2 masks
C        10.5.5.0/24 is directly connected, Loopback105
L        10.5.5.5/32 is directly connected, Loopback105
O  IA          10.6.6.0/24  [110/3]  via  10.10.10.1,  00:00:45,
FastEthernet0/0
C        10.10.10.0/24 is directly connected, FastEthernet0/0
L        10.10.10.5/32 is directly connected, FastEthernet0/0
O  IA          10.20.20.0/24  [110/2]  via  10.10.10.1,  00:00:45,
FastEthernet0/0
```

- ■ Make sure that R5 and R6 see the routes from each other as intra-area.

If the PE routers have the same OSPF domain identifier for the OSPF process facing the CE routers, then the routes will be seen by the CE routers as inter-area routes (LSA type 3). Remember that if you don't set the domain ID, the routers will use the process number as the domain ID. In this case we need the routes to be seen as intra-area routes (LSA type 1). This is trying to get us to create a sham link between the PE routers to extend the area number through the MPLS cloud.

```
R1#show run | b Loopback14
!
interface Loopback14
 vrf forwarding VPN1
 ip address 14.14.14.1 255.255.255.255
!
router ospf 2 vrf VPN1
 area 10 sham-link 14.14.14.1 14.14.14.4
 redistribute bgp 65001 subnets
 network 10.0.0.0 0.255.255.255 area 10
!
router bgp 65001
 bgp log-neighbor-changes
 neighbor 10.110.110.10 remote-as 65001
 neighbor 10.110.110.10 update-source Loopback0
 !
 address-family vpnv4
  neighbor 10.110.110.10 activate
  neighbor 10.110.110.10 send-community extended
 exit-address-family
 !
 address-family ipv4 vrf VPN1
  network 14.14.14.1 mask 255.255.255.255
  redistribute ospf 2
 exit-address-family
!
R4#show run | b Loopback14
interface Loopback14
 vrf forwarding VPN1
 ip address 14.14.14.4 255.255.255.255
!
router ospf 2 vrf VPN1
 area 10 sham-link 14.14.14.4 14.14.14.1
 redistribute bgp 65001 subnets
 network 10.0.0.0 0.255.255.255 area 10
!
router bgp 65001
```

```
 bgp log-neighbor-changes
 neighbor 10.110.110.10 remote-as 65001
 neighbor 10.110.110.10 update-source Loopback0
 !
 address-family vpnv4
  neighbor 10.110.110.10 activate
  neighbor 10.110.110.10 send-community extended
 exit-address-family
 !
 address-family ipv4 vrf VPN1
  network 14.14.14.4 mask 255.255.255.255
  redistribute ospf 2
 exit-address-family
 !
```

```
R5#show ip route
Codes: L - local, C - connected, S - static, R - RIP, M - mobile, B -
BGP
       D - EIGRP, EX - EIGRP external, O - OSPF, IA - OSPF inter area
       N1 - OSPF NSSA external type 1, N2 - OSPF NSSA external type 2
       E1 - OSPF external type 1, E2 - OSPF external type 2
       i - IS-IS, su - IS-IS summary, L1 - IS-IS level-1, L2 - IS-IS
level-2
       ia - IS-IS inter area, * - candidate default, U - per-user
static route
       o - ODR, P - periodic downloaded static route, H - NHRP, l -
LISP
       + - replicated route, % - next hop override

Gateway of last resort is not set

       10.0.0.0/8 is variably subnetted, 6 subnets, 2 masks
C        10.5.5.0/24 is directly connected, Loopback105
L        10.5.5.5/32 is directly connected, Loopback105
O              10.6.6.0/24  [110/4]  via  10.10.10.1,  00:03:56,
FastEthernet0/0
C        10.10.10.0/24 is directly connected, FastEthernet0/0
L        10.10.10.5/32 is directly connected, FastEthernet0/0
O             10.20.20.0/24  [110/3]  via  10.10.10.1,  00:03:56,
FastEthernet0/0
       14.0.0.0/32 is subnetted, 2 subnets
O E2     14.14.14.1 [110/1] via 10.10.10.1, 00:05:29, FastEthernet0/0
O E2     14.14.14.4 [110/1] via 10.10.10.1, 00:04:23, FastEthernet0/0
```

Make sure that R5 and R6 can ping others Loopback interfaces.

```
R5#ping 10.6.6.6 source loopback105
Type escape sequence to abort.
Sending 5, 100-byte ICMP Echos to 10.6.6.6, timeout is 2 seconds:
Packet sent with a source address of 10.5.5.5
!!!!!
Success  rate  is  100  percent  (5/5),  round-trip  min/avg/max  =
268/309/368 ms
R5#
```

Here are the configs for all the routers involved:

```
SW1-SW#show run
!
hostname SW1-SW
!
```

```
vtp mode transparent
!
vlan 10,15,23,46
!
interface Loopback110
 ip address 10.110.110.10 255.255.255.0
 ip ospf network point-to-point
!
interface FastEthernet1/1
 switchport access vlan 15
!
interface FastEthernet1/2
 switchport access vlan 23
!
interface FastEthernet1/3
 switchport access vlan 23
!
interface FastEthernet1/4
 switchport access vlan 46
!
interface FastEthernet1/5
 switchport access vlan 15
!
interface FastEthernet1/6
 switchport access vlan 46
!
interface Vlan23
 ip address 10.0.23.10 255.255.255.0
 mpls ip
!
router ospf 1
 log-adjacency-changes
 network 10.0.0.0 0.255.255.255 area 0
!
router bgp 65001
 no synchronization
 bgp log-neighbor-changes
 neighbor 1.1.1.1 remote-as 65001
 neighbor 1.1.1.1 update-source Loopback110
 neighbor 1.1.1.1 route-reflector-client
 neighbor 4.4.4.4 remote-as 65001
 neighbor 4.4.4.4 update-source Loopback110
 neighbor 4.4.4.4 route-reflector-client
 no auto-summary
 !
 address-family vpnv4
  neighbor 1.1.1.1 activate
  neighbor 1.1.1.1 send-community extended
  neighbor 1.1.1.1 route-reflector-client
  neighbor 4.4.4.4 activate
  neighbor 4.4.4.4 send-community extended
 exit-address-family
!
```

```
R1#show run
!
hostname R1
!
!
```

```
  rd 1:1
  route-target export 1:1
  route-target import 1:1
  !
 address-family ipv4
 exit-address-family
!
interface Loopback0
 ip address 1.1.1.1 255.255.255.0
 ip ospf network point-to-point
 !
interface Loopback14
 vrf forwarding VPN1
 ip address 14.14.14.1 255.255.255.255
 !
interface FastEthernet0/0
 vrf forwarding VPN1
 ip address 10.10.10.1 255.255.255.0
 !
interface FastEthernet0/1
 ip address 10.0.12.1 255.255.255.0
 mpls ip
 !
router ospf 2 vrf VPN1
 area 10 sham-link 14.14.14.1 14.14.14.4
 redistribute bgp 65001 subnets
 network 10.0.0.0 0.255.255.255 area 10
 !
router ospf 1
 network 1.1.1.1 0.0.0.0 area 0
 network 10.0.0.0 0.255.255.255 area 0
 !
router bgp 65001
 bgp log-neighbor-changes
 neighbor 10.110.110.10 remote-as 65001
 neighbor 10.110.110.10 update-source Loopback0
 !
 address-family vpnv4
  neighbor 10.110.110.10 activate
  neighbor 10.110.110.10 send-community extended
 exit-address-family
 !
 address-family ipv4 vrf VPN1
  network 14.14.14.1 mask 255.255.255.255
  redistribute ospf 2
 exit-address-family
!
```

```
R2#sh run
!
hostname R2
!
!
interface FastEthernet0/0
 ip address 10.0.23.2 255.255.255.0
 mpls ip
!
interface FastEthernet0/1
 ip address 10.0.12.2 255.255.255.0
 mpls ip
```

```
!
router ospf 1
 network 10.0.0.0 0.255.255.255 area 0
!
```

R3#show run
```
!
hostname R3
!
!
interface FastEthernet0/0
 ip address 10.0.23.3 255.255.255.0
 mpls ip
!
interface FastEthernet0/1
 ip address 10.0.34.3 255.255.255.0
 mpls ip
!
router ospf 1
 network 10.0.0.0 0.255.255.255 area 0
!
```

R4#show run
```
!
hostname R4
!
!
vrf definition VPN1
 rd 1:1
 route-target export 1:1
 route-target import 1:1
 !
 address-family ipv4
 exit-address-family
!
!
interface Loopback0
 ip address 4.4.4.4 255.255.255.0
 ip ospf network point-to-point
!
interface Loopback14
 vrf forwarding VPN1
 ip address 14.14.14.4 255.255.255.255
!
interface FastEthernet0/0
 vrf forwarding VPN1
 ip address 10.20.20.4 255.255.255.0
!
interface FastEthernet0/1
 ip address 10.0.34.4 255.255.255.0
 mpls ip
!
router ospf 2 vrf VPN1
 area 10 sham-link 14.14.14.4 14.14.14.1
 redistribute bgp 65001 subnets
 network 10.0.0.0 0.255.255.255 area 10
!
router ospf 1
 network 4.4.4.4 0.0.0.0 area 0
 network 10.0.0.0 0.255.255.255 area 0
```

```
router bgp 65001
 bgp log-neighbor-changes
 neighbor 10.110.110.10 remote-as 65001
 neighbor 10.110.110.10 update-source Loopback0
 !
 address-family vpnv4
  neighbor 10.110.110.10 activate
  neighbor 10.110.110.10 send-community extended
 exit-address-family
 !
 address-family ipv4 vrf VPN1
  network 14.14.14.4 mask 255.255.255.255
  redistribute ospf 2
 exit-address-family
!
```
```
R5#show run
!
hostname R5
!
interface Loopback105
 ip address 10.5.5.5 255.255.255.0
 ip ospf network point-to-point
!
interface FastEthernet0/0
 ip address 10.10.10.5 255.255.255.0
!
router ospf 1
 network 10.0.0.0 0.255.255.255 area 10
!
```
```
R6#show run
!
hostname R6
!
interface Loopback106
 ip address 10.6.6.6 255.255.255.0
 ip ospf network point-to-point
!
interface FastEthernet0/0
 ip address 10.20.20.6 255.255.255.0
!
router ospf 1
 network 10.0.0.0 0.255.255.255 area 10
!
```

Appendix B – The Lab Setup

These documents were written with the CCIE Route Switch candidate in mind. The labs within this series can be done on either a real rack of equipment or on Dynamips/GNS3. The exception would be the Layer 2 –Switching document and the switching portion of the QoS document, the "Numbers in Networking" document has no labs on equipment at all. The majority of labs are routers centric; the switches are used for interconnecting the routers. Those labs require a basic switching configuration of VLANs and possibly trunking. The lab topology used within this series is based on the Cisco 360 lab topology. The switching document and the switching portion of the QoS document do require real switches, if you do not have access to the equipment; rack rentals are available from several sources that match the 360 topology. If you are going to rack up your own, the routers can be 1900 or 2900 series or better running 15.3T Universal Software release and the switches can be wither 3560X running 15.0SE Universal (IP Services) Software release. The DMVPN switch can be any type of switch, it is not part of the required devices, but just gives Ethernet connectivity to support the DMVPN tunnels. All ports of the DMVPN switch would be in the same VLAN. So this could also just be excess ports on your other switches all in the same VLAN. The interface mapping configuration area as follows:

Table B1: Ethernet Mappings for Dynamips

Ethernet	
Router 1 FastEthernet 0/0	Switch 1 FastEthernet 0/1 (1/1 for Dynamips)
Router 1 FastEthernet 0/1	Switch 2 FastEthernet 0/1 (1/1 for Dynamips)
Router 1 FastEthernet 2/0	DMVPN Switch Port 1
Router 2 FastEthernet 0/0	Switch 1 FastEthernet 0/2 (1/2 for Dynamips)
Router 2 FastEthernet 0/1	Switch 2 FastEthernet 0/2 (1/2 for Dynamips)
Router 2 FastEthernet 2/0	DMVPN Switch Port 2
Router 3 FastEthernet 0/0	Switch 1 FastEthernet 0/3 (1/3 for Dynamips)
Router 3 FastEthernet 0/1	Switch 2 FastEthernet 0/3 (1/3 for Dynamips)
Router 3 FastEthernet 2/0	DMVPN Switch Port 3
Router 4 FastEthernet 0/0	Switch 1 FastEthernet 0/4 (1/4 for Dynamips)
Router 4 FastEthernet 0/1	Switch 2 FastEthernet 0/4 (1/4 for Dynamips)
Router 4 FastEthernet 2/0	DMVPN Switch Port 4
Router 5 FastEthernet 0/0	Switch 1 FastEthernet 0/5 (1/5 for Dynamips)
Router 5 FastEthernet 0/1	Switch 2 FastEthernet 0/5 (1/5 for Dynamips)
Router 5 FastEthernet 2/0	DMVPN Switch Port 5
Router 6 FastEthernet 0/0	Switch 1 FastEthernet 0/6 (1/6 for Dynamips)
Router 6 FastEthernet 0/1	Switch 2 FastEthernet 0/6 (1/6 for Dynamips)
Router 6 FastEthernet 2/0	DMVPN Switch Port 6

Table B2: Serial Mappings for Dynamips

Serial	
Router 1 Serial 1/0	Router 2 Serial 1/0
Router 1 Serial 1/1	Router 3 Serial 1/1
Router 2 Serial 1/0	Router 1 Serial 1/0
Router 2 Serial 1/1	Router 3 Serial 1/0
Router 3 Serial 1/0	Router 2 Serial 1/1
Router 3 Serial 1/1	Router 1 Serial 1/1
Router 4 Serial 1/0	Router 6 Serial 1/0
Router 4 Serial 1/1	Router 5 Serial 1/1
Router 5 Serial 1/0	Router 6 Serial 1/0
Router 5 Serial 1/1	Router 4 Serial 1/1
Router 6 Serial 1/0	Router 5 Serial 1/0
Router 6 Serial 1/1	Router 4 Serial 1/0

LAB Topology With Real Equipment
Ethernet Connections

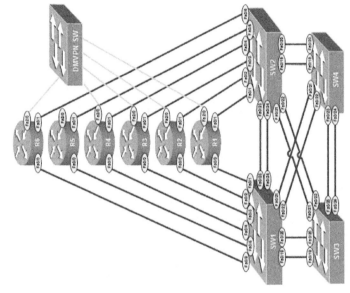

LAB Topology With Dynamips/GNS3
Ethernet Connections

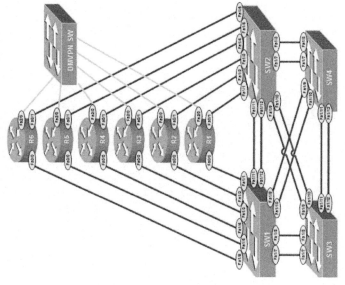

LAB Topology
Serial Connections

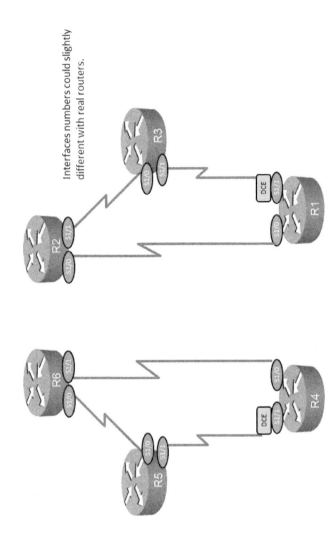

Interfaces numbers could slightly different with real routers.

GNS3 Topology

Here is the topology file I use, just replace the path to your IOS images:

autostart = False

version = 0.8.6

[127.0.0.1:7202]

  workingdir = working

  udp = 10201

  [[7200]]

    image = E:\Location of you IOS image

Stupid CCIE Tricks v5.0 - section 10: MPLS

-

```
      idlepc = 0x62f02c94
      sparsemem = True
      ghostios = True
   [[ROUTER R5]]
      console = 2105
      aux = 2505
      cnfg = configs\R5.cfg
      slot0 = C7200-IO-2FE
      f0/0 = SW1 f1/5
      f0/1 = SW2 f1/5
      slot1 = PA-8T
      s1/0 = R6 s1/0
      s1/1 = R4 s1/1
      slot2 = PA-2FE-TX
      f2/0 = DMVPN_SW 5
      x = -48.0
      y = -154.134665205
      z = 1.0
   [[ROUTER R6]]
      console = 2106
      aux = 2506
      cnfg = configs\R6.cfg
      slot0 = C7200-IO-2FE
      f0/0 = SW1 f1/6
      f0/1 = SW2 f1/6
      slot1 = PA-8T
      s1/0 = R5 s1/0
      s1/1 = R4 s1/0
      slot2 = PA-2FE-TX
      f2/0 = DMVPN_SW 6
      x = 132.0
      y = -250.134665205
      z = 1.0
[127.0.0.1:7203]
   workingdir = working
   udp = 10301
   [[3725]]
      image = E:\Location of you IOS image
      ram = 128
      idlepc = 0x60c07404
      sparsemem = True
      ghostios = True
   [[ROUTER SW1]]
      model = 3725
```

-

```
      console = 2107
      aux = 2507
      cnfg = configs\SW1.cfg
      slot1 = NM-16ESW
      f1/1 = R1 f0/0
      f1/2 = R2 f0/0
      f1/3 = R3 f0/0
      f1/4 = R4 f0/0
      f1/5 = R5 f0/0
      f1/6 = R6 f0/0
      f1/7 = SW3 f1/7
      f1/8 = SW3 f1/8
      f1/9 = SW4 f1/9
      f1/10 = SW4 f1/10
      f1/11 = SW2 f1/11
      f1/12 = SW2 f1/12
      symbol = EtherSwitch router
      x = -444.5
      y = -66.5
      z = 1.0
   [[ROUTER SW3]]
      model = 3725
      console = 2110
      aux = 2510
      cnfg = configs\SW3.cfg
      slot1 = NM-16ESW
      f1/7 = SW1 f1/7
      f1/8 = SW1 f1/8
      f1/9 = SW2 f1/9
      f1/10 = SW2 f1/10
      f1/11 = SW4 f1/11
      f1/12 = SW4 f1/12
      symbol = EtherSwitch router
      x = -448.0
      y = 79.5673326026
      z = 1.0
   [[ROUTER SW2]]
      model = 3725
      console = 2109
      aux = 2509
      cnfg = configs\SW2.cfg
      slot1 = NM-16ESW
      f1/1 = R1 f0/1
      f1/2 = R2 f0/1
```

```
      f1/3 = R3 f0/1
      f1/4 = R4 f0/1
      f1/5 = R5 f0/1
      f1/6 = R6 f0/1
      f1/7 = SW4 f1/7
      f1/8 = SW4 f1/8
      f1/9 = SW3 f1/9
      f1/10 = SW3 f1/10
      f1/11 = SW1 f1/11
      f1/12 = SW1 f1/12
      symbol = EtherSwitch router
      x = -21.5
      y = -62.5
      z = 1.0
   [[ROUTER SW4]]
      model = 3725
      console = 2111
      aux = 2511
      cnfg = configs\SW4.cfg
      slot1 = NM-16ESW
      f1/7 = SW2 f1/7
      f1/8 = SW2 f1/8
      f1/9 = SW1 f1/9
      f1/10 = SW1 f1/10
      f1/11 = SW3 f1/11
      f1/12 = SW3 f1/12
      symbol = EtherSwitch router
      x = -22.0
      y = 86.4326673974
      z = 1.0
[127.0.0.1:7200]
   workingdir = working
   udp = 10001
   [[7200]]
      image = E:\Location of you IOS image
      idlepc = 0x62f02c94
      sparsemem = True
      ghostios = True
   [[ROUTER R1]]
      console = 2101
      aux = 2501
      cnfg = configs\R1.cfg
      slot0 = C7200-IO-2FE
      f0/0 = SW1 f1/1
```

```
      f0/1 = SW2 f1/1
      slot1 = PA-8T
      s1/0 = R2 s1/0
      s1/1 = R3 s1/1
      slot2 = PA-2FE-TX
      f2/0 = DMVPN_SW 1
      x = -651.0
      y = -250.0
      z = 1.0
   [[ROUTER R2]]
      console = 2102
      aux = 2502
      cnfg = configs\R2.cfg
      slot0 = C7200-IO-2FE
      f0/0 = SW1 f1/2
      f0/1 = SW2 f1/2
      slot1 = PA-8T
      s1/0 = R1 s1/0
      s1/1 = R3 s1/0
      slot2 = PA-2FE-TX
      f2/0 = DMVPN_SW 2
      x = -509.0
      y = -169.865334795
      z = 1.0
   [[ETHSW DMVPN_SW]]
      1 = access 1 R1 f2/0
      2 = access 1 R2 f2/0
      3 = access 1 R3 f2/0
      4 = access 1 R4 f2/0
      5 = access 1 R5 f2/0
      6 = access 1 R6 f2/0
      x = -184.5
      y = -362.0
      z = 1.0
[127.0.0.1:7201]
   workingdir = working
   udp = 10101
   [[7200]]
      image = E:\Location of you IOS image
      idlepc = 0x62f02c94
      sparsemem = True
      ghostios = True
   [[ROUTER R4]]
      console = 2104
```

```
        aux = 2504
        cnfg = configs\R4.cfg
        slot0 = C7200-IO-2FE
        f0/0 = SW1 f1/4
        f0/1 = SW2 f1/4
        slot1 = PA-8T
        s1/0 = R6 s1/1
        s1/1 = R5 s1/1
        slot2 = PA-2FE-TX
        f2/0 = DMVPN_SW 4
        x = -202.0
        y = -255.0
        z = 1.0
    [[ROUTER R3]]
        console = 2103
        aux = 2503
        cnfg = configs\R3.cfg
        slot0 = C7200-IO-2FE
        f0/0 = SW1 f1/3
        f0/1 = SW2 f1/3
        slot1 = PA-8T
        s1/0 = R2 s1/1
        s1/1 = R1 s1/1
        slot2 = PA-2FE-TX
        f2/0 = DMVPN_SW 3
        x = -327.0
        y = -223.865334795
        z = 1.0
[GNS3-DATA]
    configs = configs
    workdir = working
```

Appendix C - IPv6 over MPLS

This section was written up before the version 5 was released. Rather than throwing it out, some my find it useful for the version 5 written or for the CCIE Service Provider.

As of this writing, the native support of MPLS with IPv6 has not yet been ratified. There is a draft RFC for LDP-IPv6 (https://tools.ietf.org/html/draft-ietf-mpls-ldp-ipv6-12) that expires in August of 2014. That draft RFC proposes to modify RFC 5036 (*LDP Specifications*) to allow for native LDP support with IPv4, IPv6 or both. At this point, the only option for IPv6 and MPLS is to run MPLS with IPv4 and then carry IPv6 routes and payload over MPLS.   That process can be one as a single tunnel between PE routers (6PE) or multiple tunnels using Layer 3 VPNs between PEs (6VPE).

6PE and 6VPE

There are two RFCs that define transporting IPv6 over MPLS:
- RFC 4798: IPv6 provider edge router (6PE) over MPLS
- RFC 4659: IPv6 VPN provider edge (6VPE) over MPLS

In both cases, the core runs IPv4 at the control plane (plus label control for MPLS forwarding). The dual stack PE router is then encapsulating the IPv6 packet into MPLS header for 6PE, the VPNv6 prefix plus label for 6VPE. The VPNv6 prefix is an IPv6 address prepended with an 8 byte route distinguisher.

Before the IPv6 Provider Edge Router over MPLS (6PE) or IPv6 Provider Edge Router ospf MPLS VPN (6VPE) features can be implemented, MPLS must be running over the core IPv4 network with all IPv4 supporting protocols (LDPv4, TEv4, IGPv4, MP-BGP).

Configuring 6PE

All that's need to add IPv6 support to a PE router (already configured as an IPv4 PE with an iBGP relationship with another PE router, and with MPLS and LDP running) is to add the **neighbor send-label** command under the address family IPv6.

```
router bgp 100
 bgp router-id 200.10.10.1
 no synchronization
```

```
 neighbor 2001:DB8:1::1 remote-as 65014
 neighbor 2001:DB8:1::1 description CustomerA
 neighbor 200.10.10.2 remote-as 100
 neighbor 200.10.10.2 description PE2
 neighbor 200.10.10.2 update-source Loopback0
!
 address-family ipv6
  neighbor 200.10.10.2 activate
  neighbor 200.10.10.2 send-label
  neighbor 2001:DB8:1::1 activate
  redistribute connected
  exit-address-family
```

Configuring 6VPE

As with the Layer 3 VPN for IPv4, we need to involve Virtual Routing and
Forwarding (VRF) tables for 6VPE. The VRF syntax has been modified slightly to
support multiple protocols (IPv4 and IPv6). Use the **vrf definition** command from
the global configuration mode to enter the VRF configuration mode. Within the
VRF configuration mode, configure the route distinguisher; then identify the
address family or families. Under the address family, you would configure the
route targets. You apply the VRF to an interface using the **vrf forward** command.
Note: To support both IPv4 and IPv6, the **IP** keyword was dropped from the
syntax.

```
vrf definition CustomerA
 rd 200:1
!
address-family ipv6
  route-target export 200:1
  route-target import 200:1
  exit-address-family
!
interface FastEthernet0/0
 Description Link to CE1
 vrf forwarding CustomerA
 ipv6 address 2001:db8:cafe:1::1/64
```

As in VRF Lite for IPv4, you have the option of different routing context for each
VRF. RIPng is the only routing protocol that does not support VRFs (as of these
writing).
For a static IPv6 routes, use the **ipv6 route** command in global configuration
mode.

ipv6 route vrf vrf-name ipv6-prefix/prefix-length { ipv6-address |
interface-type interface-number [**ipv6-address**] } [**nexthop-vrf** [vrf-
name1 **| default**]] [administrative-distance] [administrative-multicast-
distance **| unicast | multicast**] [next-hop-address] [**tag** tag] [**name**
name]

ipv6-prefix	The IPv6 network that is the destination of the static route. Can also be a host name when static host routes are configured.
/ prefix-length	The length of the IPv6 prefix. A decimal value that indicates how many of the high-order contiguous bits of the address comprise the prefix (the network portion of the address). A slash mark must precede the decimal value.
vrf	Specifies all virtual private network (VPN) routing/forwarding instance (VRF) tables or a specific VRF table for IPv4 or IPv6 address.
vrf-name	Names a specific VRF table for an IPv4 or IPv6 address.
ipv6-address	The IPv6 address of the next hop that can be used to reach the specified network. The IPv6 address of the next hop need not be directly connected; recursion is done to find the IPv6 address of the directly connected next hop. When an interface type and interface number are specified, you can optionally specify the IPv6 address of the next hop to which packets are output. Note — You must specify an interface type and an interface number when using a link-local address as the next hop (the link-local next hop must also be an adjacent device). This argument must be in the form documented in RFC 2373 where the address is specified in hexadecimal using 16-bit values between colons.
interface-type	Interface type. For more information about supported interface types, use the question mark (?) online help function. You can use the *interface-type* argument to direct static routes out point-to-point interfaces (such as serial or tunnel interfaces) and broadcast interfaces (such as Ethernet interfaces). When using the *interface-type* argument with point-to-point interfaces, there is no need to specify the IPv6 address of the next hop. When using the *interface-type* argument with broadcast interfaces, you should always specify the IPv6 address of the next hop or ensure that the specified prefix is assigned to the link. A link-local address should be

	specified as the next hop for broadcast interfaces.
interface-number	Interface number. For more information about the numbering syntax for supported interface types, use the question mark (?) online help function.
nexthop-vrf	(Optional) Indicator that the next hop is a VRF.
vrf-name1	(Optional) Name of the next-hop VRF.
default	(Optional) Indicator that the next hop is the default.
administrative-distance	(Optional) An administrative distance. The default value is 1, which gives static routes precedence over any other type of route except connected routes.
administrative-multicast-distance	(Optional) The distance used when selecting this route for multicast Reverse Path Forwarding (RPF).
unicast	(Optional) Specifies a route that must not be used in multicast RPF selection.
multicast	(Optional) Specifies a route that must not be populated in the unicast Routing Information Base (RIB).
next-hop-address	(Optional) Address of the next hop that can be used to reach the specified network.
tag *tag*	(Optional) Tag value that can be used as a "match" value for controlling redistribution via route maps.
name route-name	(Optional) Specifies a name for the route.

For Open Shortest Path First version 3 (OSPFv3), use the **address-family ipv6 vrf** command in router configuration mode.

address-family ipv6 [unicast] vrf *vrf-name*

unicast	(Optional) Specifies IPv6 unicast address prefixes.
vrf *vrf-name*	Specifies the name of the VPN routing and forwarding (VRF) instance to associate with subsequent IPv4 address family configuration mode commands.

For Enhanced Interior Gateway Routing Protocol (EIGRP) the named EGIRP process, then use the **address-family ipv6 vrf autonomous-system** command in the router configuration mode.

address-family ipv6 [unicast] [vrf *vrf-name*] autonomous-system *autonomous-system-number*

ipv6	Selects the IPV6 protocol address-family. IPv6 is supported only in EIGRP named configurations.
multicast	(Optional) Specifies the multicast address-family. This keyword is available only in EIGRP

	named IPv4 configurations.
unicast	(Optional) Specifies the unicast address-family.
autonomous-system autonomous-system-number	(Optional) Specifies the autonomous system number. This keyword/argument pair is required for EIGRP named configurations.
vrf vrf-name	Specifies the name of the VRF. This keyword/argument pair is required for EIGRP AS configurations.

For BGP, first place the router in address family configuration mode for configuring routing sessions, that use standard VPNv6 address prefixes, use the **address-family vpnv6** command in router configuration mode. There you will need to activate the other PE router via its IPv4 address. Don't forget to send communities as well (if the router doesn't add that command for you).

Then enter the address family vrf configuration mode for configuring routing sessions, such as BGP or redistribution, that use standard IPv6 address prefixes, use the **address-family ipv6 vrf** command in router configuration mode.

```
router bgp 100
 neighbor 200.10.10.2 remote-as 100
 neighbor 200.10.10.2 description PE2
 neighbor 200.10.10.2 update-source lo0
!
address-family vpnv6
  neighbor 200.10.10.2 activate
  neighbor 200.10.10.2 send-community ext
  exit-address-family
!
 address-family ipv6 vrf CustomerA
  neighbor 2001:db8:cafe:1::1 remote-as 500
  neighbor 2001:db8:cafe:1::1 activate
  redistribute connected
  redistribute static
  exit-address-family
```

To verify the configuration, use the **show bgp vpnv6 unicast vrf** and/or **show ipv6 cef vrf** commands to display what routes are learned and forwarded. Both commands will also show if there are labels in use for the routes.